ZONI
ENGLISH SYSTEM
A Unique Classroom Instructional Method™

The Zoni English System

1

Second Edition

Methodology:	**Pat Ossa** **Zoilo C. Nieto**
Editor:	**Keith W. Hansen, Ph.D.**
Director:	**Zoilo C. Nieto**

Foreword

The Zoni English System has been designed as a classroom instructional method in response to the demonstrated great needs of nonnative speakers of English in everyday life in English-speaking countries.

Since communication is essential for survival, *The Zoni English System* method is based on daily life situations while explaining fundamental expressions as well as grammatical structures. In so doing, we have also employed a high-frequency vocabulary. An effective textual material increases the student's motivation to continue studying English by influencing his or her attitude toward learning as well as enhancing his or her future possibilities.

Objectives
The Zoni English System achieves these objectives:
1. To reach out to accommodate students of diverse backgrounds
2. To create a universal program for anyone who wants to learn practical English
3. To make students think in English
4. To encourage students to lose any fear of the language
5. To keep student motivation high in the learning process
6. To build up students' fluency

The Zoni English System 1 features 9 lessons:

- It begins with an essential, conversational exercise in order to "break the ice." This exercise facilitates the introduction of fundamental expressions and basic structures as well as the development of subsequent lessons.
- Lessons 2-5 introduce and develop the verb "to be," demonstrative adjectives, time and time expressions and possessives.

- Lessons 6-9 concentrate on the simple present tense, there is/there are, how much/how many and basic prepositions.

TO THE TEACHER

<u>In the classroom</u>
Teacher talking time 25%
Student talking time 75%

Techniques to be employed:

Instructors utilize such teaching techniques as:
- C.I.P.: Choral Intonation Practice
- Backward build-up (expansion) drill
- Elicitation
- Vanishing
- Interaction
- Role playing
- Using commands to direct behavior
- Action sequence
- Getting students to practice self-correction
- Conversation practice
- Single-slot substitution drills
- Multiple-slot substitution drills
- Chain drills
- Transformation drills
- Teacher's silence
- Word charts
- Structured feedback
- Positive suggestion
- Question and answer exercises
- Language games: information gap, choice, feedback, party time
  (See the Zoni Teacher's Manual.)
- Fill-in-the-blank exercises
- Peripheral learning
- Dictation (find scripts in the Zoni Teacher's Manual.)

Lesson plan/technique explanations are available for instructors.

For teachers that have not gone through the Zoni co-teaching program, the methodology and techniques detailed in the **Zoni Teacher's Manual** must be followed.

Important symbols: They are found throughout the book.

When you see these symbols, use the substitution drill. This will encourage students to enrich their vocabulary by using various nouns, adjectives, verbs, etc.

Teachers have to continue eliciting to complete the interaction with the entire class participating.

Teachers have to make groups of 2 students for the Pair Practice period.

Teachers ask students to stand up and to perform their dialogues.

Classroom Seating Arrangements

In addition to teachers' varying their teaching routines, we also encourage teachers to vary their classroom seating arrangements based on what is being taught. The seating arrangements will depend upon the number of students and classroom size.

Standard

This type of seating arrangement, where students are arranged in rows, is generally used for lecture-type lessons and presentations. It is also beneficial when we need all the students to be focused on a particular task on the board. Students are able to work at their own pace doing their work. It tends to be teacher-centered. The teacher must circulate and have lots of eye contact with his/her students to make sure all are involved.

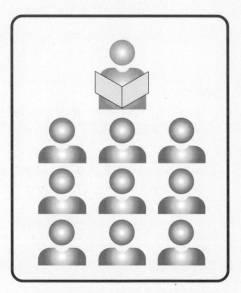

In the Zoni System, we generally begin with this seating arrangement when introducing a grammar point.

Semi-circle

This seating arrangement is recommended when we want to have maximum student interaction while focused on a particular task such as getting information from the board, watching a video or listening to a tape. Students are able to see their classmates' body and facial expressions easily during the discussions. It is less teacher-centered, so there is a lot of student interaction.

Circle: group work

Group work generally consists of three or more students. There is maximum student participation. Students are more relaxed about experimenting with the language, and the fear of making a mistake is diminished. Group work is a cooperative learning experience where students not only learn from their teacher but also from their classmates.

Pair work

The same conditions exist as with group work but with 2 students.

In the lower levels, the Zoni System incorporates a lot of group work and/or pair work during the Practice Period sessions.

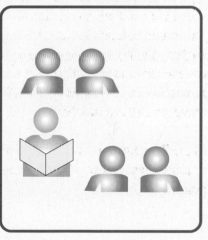

Homework

When we assign homework to students, it is important that we also check their homework in the following class. Checking homework should not take more than 15 minutes. Make sure you check all students' homework. Vary your checking homework routine; for example, check homework in the second hour of class. Finally, keep a record of which students have not done their homework. For each homework assignment not completed, a student gets a zero. Warn the student that should s/he get a lot of homework zeroes, s/he may have to repeat the course.

Surprise Factor

Though developing a routine in the classroom is good, at other times, it is critical that teachers change their classroom routines to keep students on their toes.

Some examples in using the surprise factor are:

1. Checking the homework in the second hour of the class period instead of at the beginning of the class period.
2. Asking the class a question, then zeroing in and calling on a student to answer it.

Indispensable Oral Practice

The command "listen and repeat" is found throughout the book. This technique consists of the presentation of semantic illustrations and graphics that the instructor demonstrates and to which the students respond. In addition to the use of question and answer sessions, *The Zoni English System* encourages choral and individual repetition in order to improve the student's pronunciation and to lose any fear of the language. The heading "Oral Practice" also appears throughout each lesson. These exercises should be practiced at least twice, using choral and/or individual participation.

Elicit from the Students

Elicit all vocabulary and examples from the students. Take advantage of students' prior knowledge. By doing so, we share their knowledge with the rest of the class, build confidence, promote active thinking and stimulate students to come up with interesting examples in the dialogues.

Vocabulary

A vocabulary page is found in the Zoni Teacher's Manual for each lesson. It is advisable to introduce vocabulary in context; therefore, instructors should be aware of the vocabulary and present and explain it, in context, when the right moment arises.

Board Work

At Zoni, we believe in keeping the board work as simple as possible, especially when teaching the beginner and intermediate levels. Board work is beneficial in that teachers can use it as a resource for student practice when doing Choral Intonation Practice (CIP), drilling and role playing. Board work keeps students focused. Board work reinforces reading and spelling.

While doing board work, make sure *all* students have their books and notebooks *closed*. *No* writing or copying is allowed during this period. All students must be focused on the board. Write in print, not script. Plan ahead what you will be putting on the board. If writing a long dialogue, work your dialogue one segment at a time. We strongly recommend that teachers follow our board work examples seen in the Zoni Teacher's Manual.

Attendance

Learning English is a matter of constant, consistent practice and dedication. Student attendance is vital for maximum learning and benefits; this is why teachers must remind students that regular attendance is necessary. If students do not comply, they may be asked to take the course again. Attendance should not be taken for granted. Encouragement and reminders about class attendance are essential.

Acknowledgments

I'm proud to see the publication of the revised and updated second edition of our textbook and teaching tool, *Zoni English System 1*. A large number of people have been involved in this project; it is due to their passion, persistent dedication and cooperation that this improved *Zoni English System 1* has been completed. I would like to give special thanks to **Masami Soeda** for her outstanding graphic-design work. I would also like to thank the Zoni faculty for their cooperation and suggestions; in particular, I want to thank **Ms. Millie Agostino** for her input. And I want to recognize the contributions from Zoni Language Centers students who have provided us with much-needed feedback.

Zoilo C. Nieto
Director

CONTENTS

Nice to meet you!

Lesson 1

Greetings
Alphabet
Human body
Numbers
Days/Months
Colors

Essential Conversation

ZONI ENGLISH SYSTEM ©

Alphabet

(Listen and repeat)

A a	B b	C c	D d	E e	F f	G g
H h	I i	J j	K k	L l	M m	N n
O o	P p	Q q	R r	S s	T t	U u
	V v	W w	X x	Y y	Z z	

Vowels   a   e   i   o   u

Consonants   b c d f g h j k l m n
p q r s t v w x y z

Pronunciation Practice

b	v
s	x
c	z
y	u
k	q

g	j
m	n
e	i
a	e

Homework

Write the alphabet.

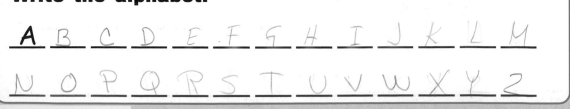

A B C D E F G H I J K L M

N O P Q R S T U V W X Y Z

ZONI ENGLISH SYSTEM ©

Essential Conversation
(Listen and repeat)

What's your name?

My name is Marisol.

Spell it, please.

M-a-r-i-s-o-l.

Student A

Student B

Writing Exercise

What's your name?

My name is María.

Spell it, please.

M-A-R-I-A

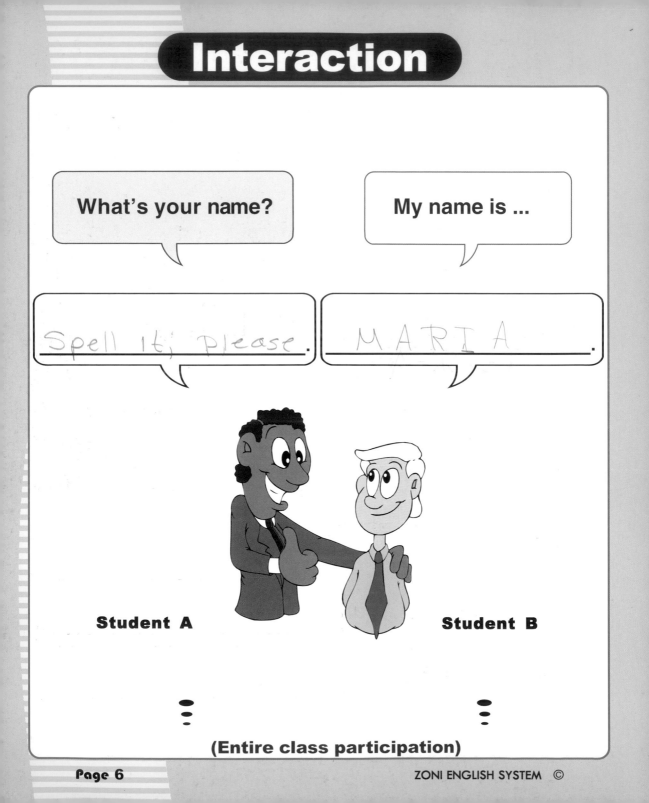

Essential Conversation

(Listen and repeat)

What's your last name?

My last name is Garcia.

Spell It, please.

G - a - r - c - i - a.

Student A

Student B

Writing Exercise

What's your last name? — My last name is García.

Spell it, please. — G-A-R-C-I-A

Interaction

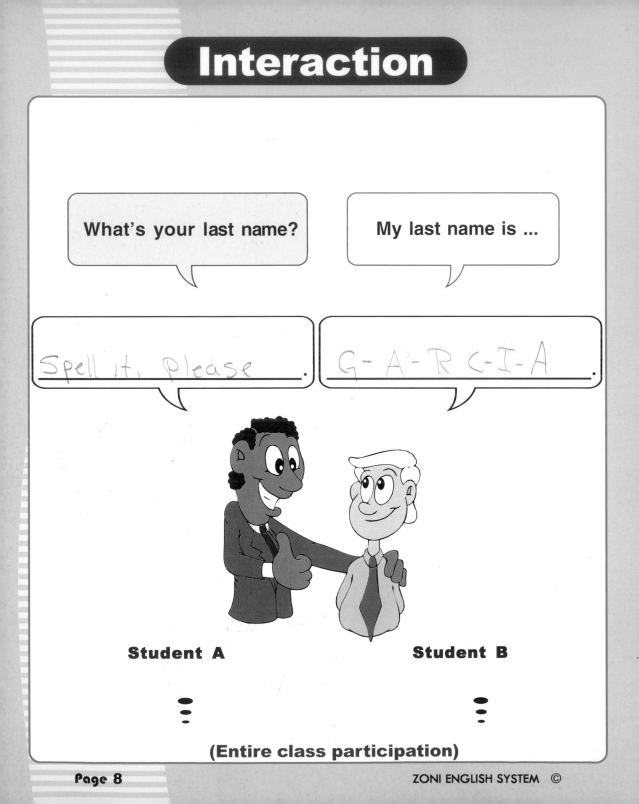

ZONI ENGLISH SYSTEM ©

The Human Body
(Listen and repeat)

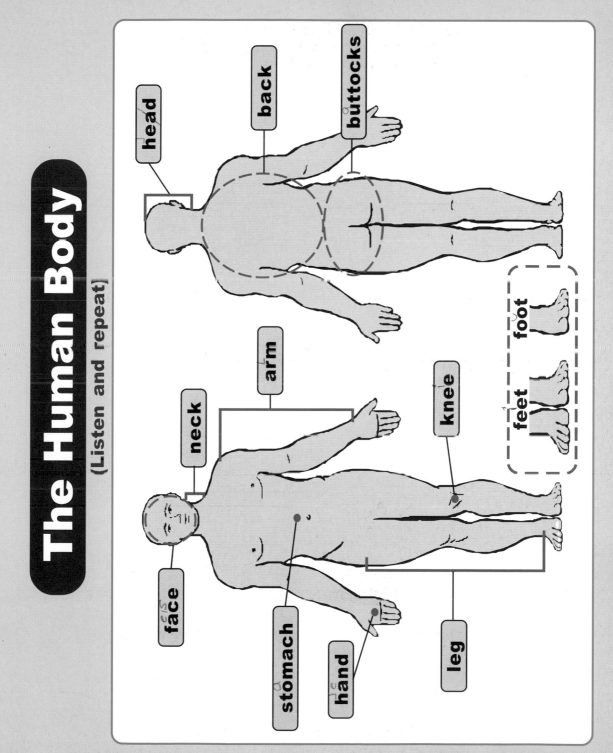

head

back

buttocks

arm

neck

knee

face

stomach

hand

leg

foot

feet

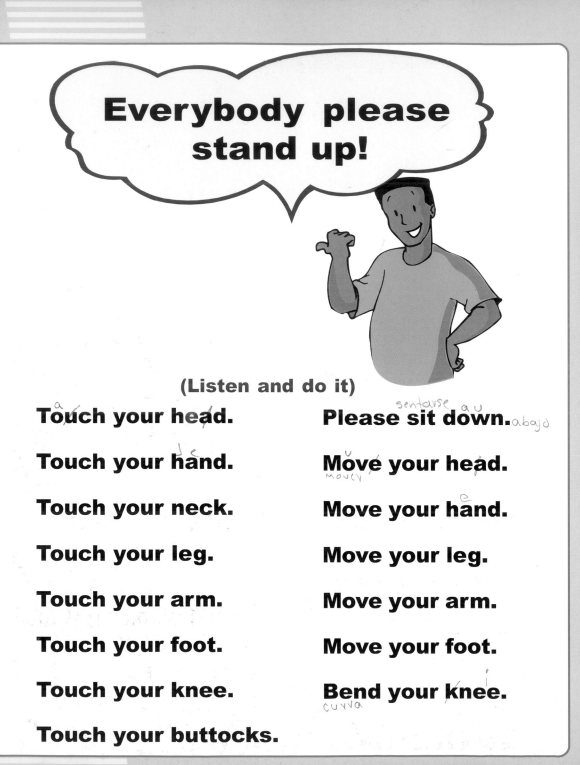

Everybody please stand up!

(Listen and do it)

Touch your head.	Please sit down.
Touch your hand.	Move your head.
Touch your neck.	Move your hand.
Touch your leg.	Move your leg.
Touch your arm.	Move your arm.
Touch your foot.	Move your foot.
Touch your knee.	Bend your knee.
Touch your buttocks.	

ZONI ENGLISH SYSTEM ©

Expressions

(Listen and repeat)

Numbers
(Listen and repeat)

money	check	ruler	calculator

0 - zero		
1 - one	11 - eleven	21 - twenty-one
2 - two	12 - twelve	22 - twenty-two
3 - three	13 - thirteen	⋮ ⋮
4 - four	14 - fourteen	30 - thirty
5 - five	15 - fifteen	40 - forty
6 - six	16 - sixteen	50 - fifty
7 - seven	17 - seventeen	60 - sixty
8 - eight	18 - eighteen	70 - seventy
9 - nine	19 - nineteen	80 - eighty
10 - ten	20 - twenty	90 - ninety

Exercise — Write the numbers in letters.

1 _____one_____   30 _Thirty_   17 _Seventeen_

60 _Sixty_   13 _Thirteen_   9 _nine_

Pronunciation Practice

13	30	15	50	17	70
14	40	16	60	18	80

ZONI ENGLISH SYSTEM ©

The teacher asks students to count ...

pregunta

a contar

(Listen and do it)

Please count to 7.

Please count to 10.

Please count to 3.

Please count to 12.

Please count backwards from 4.

hacia atrás

Please count backwards from 8.

Please count backwards from 14.

Please count backwards from 20.

Essential Conversation
(Listen and repeat)

Como viejo
How old are you?

I'm 34 years old.

Student A   Student B

Homework

verk
deberes

How old are you?

I'm 42 years old.

ZONI ENGLISH SYSTEM ©

Interaction

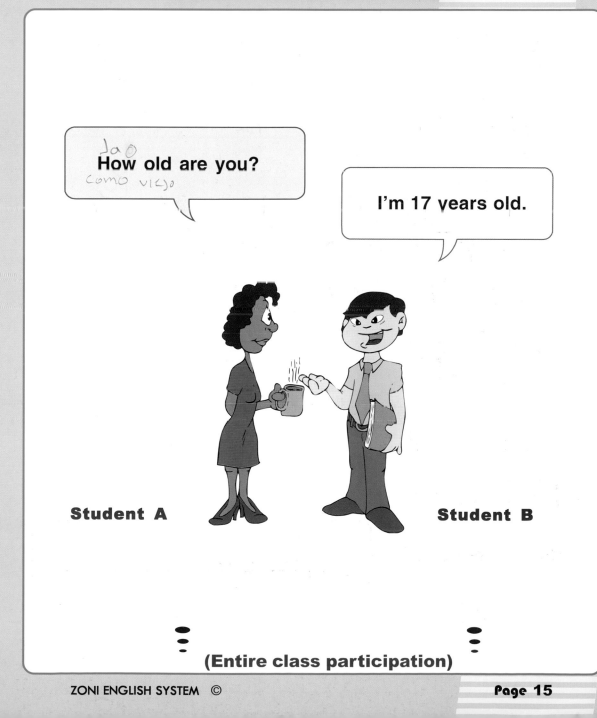

Essential Conversation

What's your phone number?

My phone number is area code (212) 651-4968.

Student A

Student B

Homework

What's your phone number?

My phone number is area code (212) 541-6906

Interaction

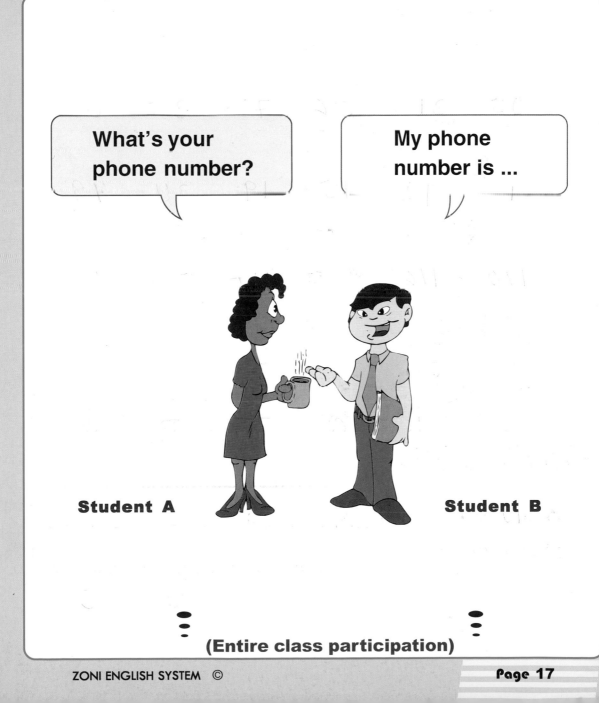

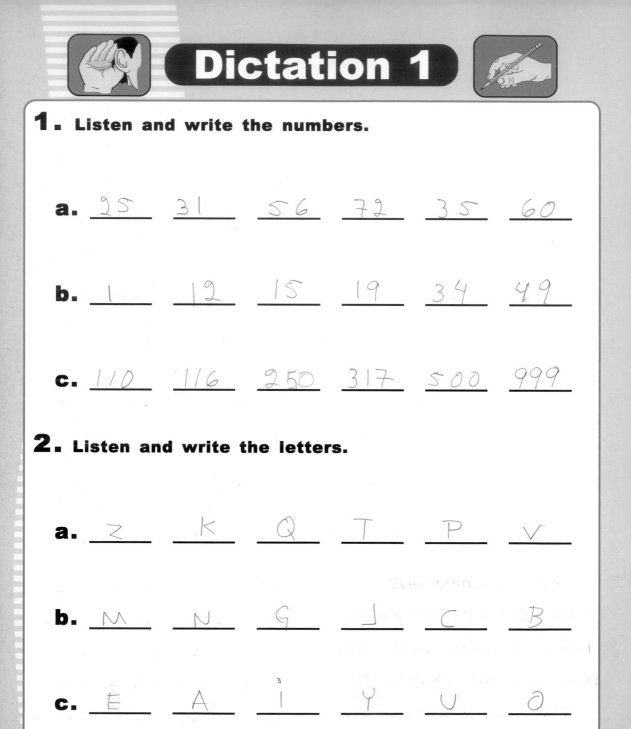

Dictation 1

1. **Listen and write the numbers.**

a. 25   31   56   72   35   60

b. 1   12   15   19   34   49

c. 110   116   250   317   500   999

2. **Listen and write the letters.**

a. Z   K   Q   T   P   V

b. M   N   G   J   C   B

c. E   A   I   Y   U   O

ZONI ENGLISH SYSTEM ©

Days of the Week

(Listen and repeat)

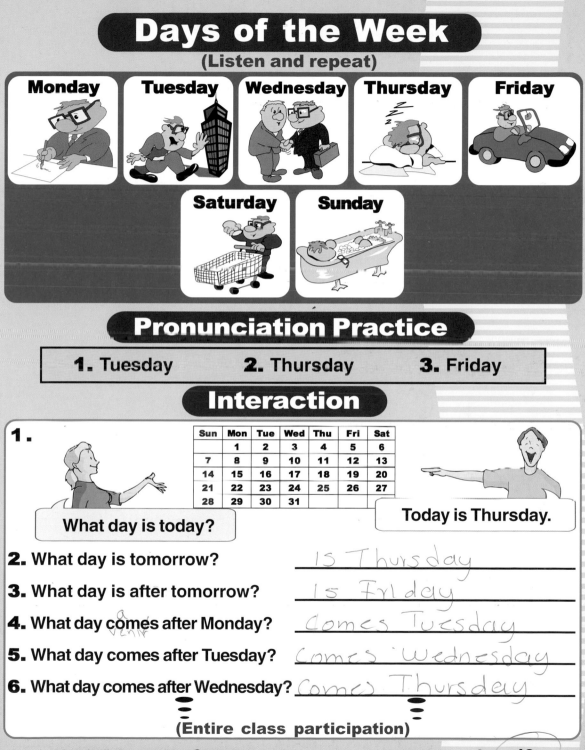

Monday

Tuesday

Wednesday

Thursday

Friday

Saturday

Sunday

Pronunciation Practice

1. Tuesday   **2.** Thursday   **3.** Friday

Interaction

1.

Sun	Mon	Tue	Wed	Thu	Fri	Sat
	1	2	3	4	5	6
7	8	9	10	11	12	13
14	15	16	17	18	19	20
21	22	23	24	25	26	27
28	29	30	31			

What day is today?

Today is Thursday.

2. What day is tomorrow? _Is Thursday_

3. What day is after tomorrow? _Is Friday_

4. What day comes after Monday? _comes Tuesday_

5. What day comes after Tuesday? _comes Wednesday_

6. What day comes after Wednesday? _comes Thursday_

(Entire class participation)

Months of the Year
(Listen and repeat)

January	February	March	April	May	June

July	August	September	October	November	December

Pronunciation Practice

1. January   **2.** February   **3.** April

4. July   **5.** August   **6.** birthday

Interaction

1. What month is Halloween in?

OCT 31

Halloween is in October.

2. What month is your birthday in? _birthday is in August_

3. What month is Valentine's Day in? _Valentine's is in February_

4. What month is Christmas in? _Christmas is in December_

5. What month is Thanksgiving in? _Thanksgiving is in November_

6. What month is Independence Day in? _Independence is in July_

(Entire class participation)

ZONI ENGLISH SYSTEM ©

Homework

Exercise A — Write the months of the year.

(gait)
escribir

January	February	March	April	May	June
January	February	March	April	May	June
January	February	March	April	May	June
January	February	March	April	May	June

July	August	September	October	November	December
July	August	September	October	November	December
July	August	September	October	November	December
July	Agust	September	October	November	December

Exercise B — Write the days of the week.

Monday	Tuesday	Wednesday	Thursday	Friday	Saturday	Sunday
Monday	Tuesday	Wednesday	Thursday	Friday	Saturday	Sunday
Monday	Tuesday	Wednesday	Thursday	Friday	Saturday	Sunday
Monday	Tuesday	Wednesday	Thursday	Friday	Saturday	Sunday
Monday	Tuesday	Wednesday	Thursday	Friday	Saturday	Sunday
Monday	Tuesday	Wednesday	Thursday	Friday	Saturday	Sunday

Essential Conversation

(Listen and repeat)

Hi.

Hi. How are you?

Fine, thank you. And you?

Fine, thanks. Where are you from?

I'm from Korea.

Where in Korea?

Seoul.

Student A

Student B

ZONI ENGLISH SYSTEM ©

Interaction

Hi.

Hi. How are you?

Fine, thank you. _And you_?

Fine, thanks. _Where are you from_?

I'm from Mexico. _Where in México_?

San Luis Potosi.

Student A

Student B

(Entire class participation)

Colors in the Classroom

(Listen and repeat)

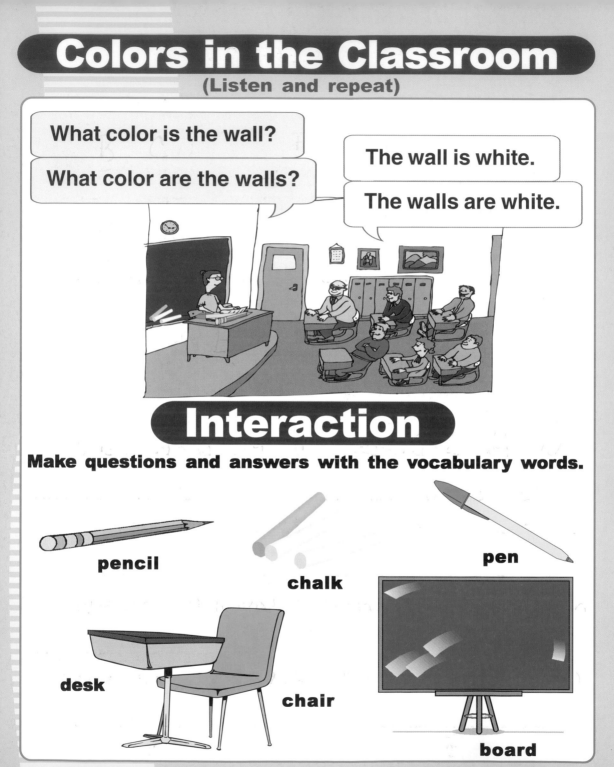

What color is the wall?

What color are the walls?

The wall is white.

The walls are white.

Interaction

Make questions and answers with the vocabulary words.

pencil

chalk

pen

desk

chair

board

Colors

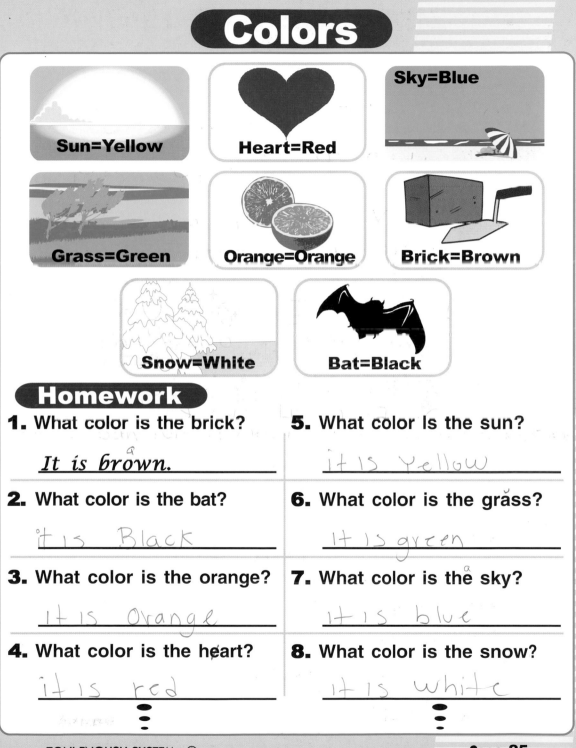

Sun=Yellow

Heart=Red

Sky=Blue

Grass=Green

Orange=Orange

Brick=Brown

Snow=White

Bat=Black

Homework

1. What color is the brick?

It is brown.

2. What color is the bat?

it is Black

3. What color is the orange?

It is Orange

4. What color is the heart?

it is red

5. What color Is the sun?

it is Yellow

6. What color is the grass?

It is green

7. What color is the sky?

it is blue

8. What color is the snow?

it is white

Homework

Exercise A   Complete the alphabet.

A B C D E F G H I J K
L M N O P Q R S T U
V W X Y Z

Exercise B   Write the vowels.

A   E   I   O   U

Exercise C   Write the consonants.

B C D F G H J K L M N
P Q R S T V W X Y Z

Exercise D   Write the numbers in letters.

12 Twelve   20 Twenty   9 nine   18 eighteen

21 Twenty one 30 Thirty 29 Twenty nine 14 Fourteen

0 Zero   13 Thirteen   6 six   11 Eleven

ZONI ENGLISH SYSTEM ©

Exercise E — Practice writing the following numbers.

12 twelve	**13** thirteen	**30** thirty	**5** five
twelve	thirteen	thirty	Five
twelve	thirteen	thirty	Five
Twelve	thirteen	Thirty	Five
Twelve	thirteen	Thirty	Five
Twelve	thirteen	thirty	Five
Twelve	thirteen	thirty	Five
Twelve	Thirteen	Thirty	Five

Exercise F — Practice writing the following vocabulary.

1. name	**2. last name**	**3. telephone number**
name	last name	Telephone number
name	last name	Telephon number
name	last name	Telephon number
name	last name	Telephon number
name	last name	Telephon number
name	last name	Telephon number
name	last name	Telephon number

Oral Exam

Student A

Student B

A: Hi. How are you?

B: Fine, thank you. And you?

A: Fine, thanks. My name is George. What's your name?

B: My name is Susan.

A: What's your last name?

B: My last name is Martinez.

A: Spell it, please.

B: M-A-R-T-I-N-E-Z

A: Where are you from?

B: I'm from Mexico.

A: Where in Mexico?

B: Puebla.

A: What's your phone number?

B: My phone number is area code (212) 460-5050. _541 6906_

A: How old are you?

B: I'm 19 years old.

A: What day is today?

B: Today is ___Thursday___.

A: What month is your birthday in?

B: My birthday is in October.

A: What color is the wall?

B: The wall is white.

A: Nice to meet you.

B: Nice to meet you, too.

ZONI ENGLISH SYSTEM ©

Lesson 2

How's the weather?

A/An
Pronunciation
How do you say this?
What do you do?
Verb "to be"
Adjectives
How's the weather?

$$\boxed{\begin{array}{c} \text{A} \\ \text{An} \end{array} = 1}$$

(Listen and repeat)

A

1. A <u>p</u>enny

3. A <u>b</u>ox

5. A <u>t</u>elevision

7. A <u>c</u>omputer

An

2. An <u>i</u>ron

4. An <u>a</u>irplane

6. An <u>e</u>lephant

8. An <u>o</u>range

Exercise   Use **A** or **An**

1. a Bank

2. a computer

3. an airplane

4. a train

5. an elephant

6. a door

7. a bird

8. a quarter

9. a newspaper

10. an apple

11. a pencil

12. a check

ZONI ENGLISH SYSTEM ©

Page 31

Game
Everybody stand up

Students imagine the objects.

1.

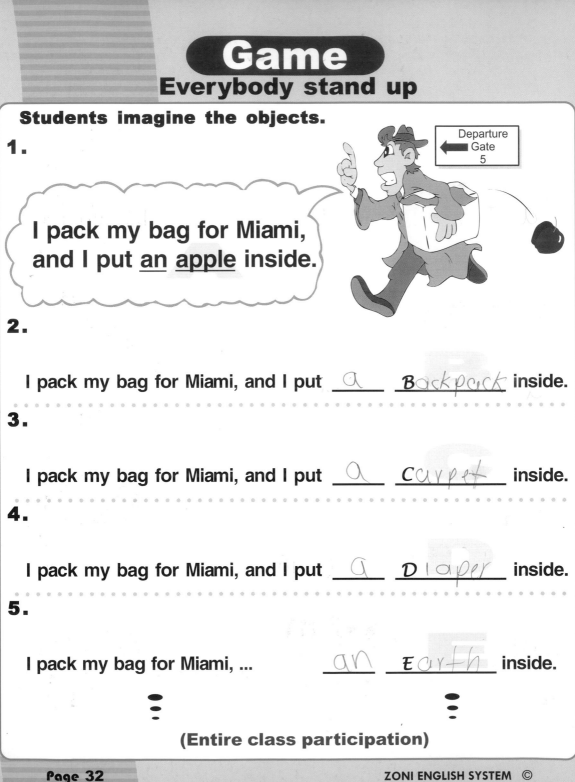

I pack my bag for Miami, and I put <u>an apple</u> inside.

Departure Gate 5

2.

I pack my bag for Miami, and I put ___a___ ___Backpack___ inside.

3.

I pack my bag for Miami, and I put ___a___ ___carpet___ inside.

4.

I pack my bag for Miami, and I put ___a___ ___Diaper___ inside.

5.

I pack my bag for Miami, ... ___an___ ___Earth___ inside.

(Entire class participation)

ZONI ENGLISH SYSTEM ©

Pronunciation

(Listen and repeat)

A t**a**pe   c**a**t

E f**ee**t   p**e**n

I f**i**re   p**i**ll

O s**o**ap   p**o**t

U m**u**sic   **u**mbrella

Excuse me.
How do you say this _____ in English?

<u>A</u> <u>book</u>.

A: Excuse me. How do you say this _____ in English?

B: *An apple*.

A: Excuse me. How do you say this _____ in English?

B: A hand

Students ask the teacher questions.

?

(Entire class participation)

1.

I'm <u>a</u> <u>teacher</u>.

2.

A: What do you do?

B: I'm ___a___ ___plumber___.

3.

C: What do you do?

D: I'm ___A___ ___singer___.

Jobs

a	teacher
a	plumber
a	doctor
a	mehanic
a	reporter
a	writer
a	miusical
a	mum
a	dentist
a	mailcarrier
a	curpenter
a	secretary
a	cook
a	plumer
a	halrstylist
a	waiter

Personal Pronouns

(Listen and repeat)

Singular	Plural

ZONI ENGLISH SYSTEM ©

Verb to be
Affirmative
(Listen and repeat)

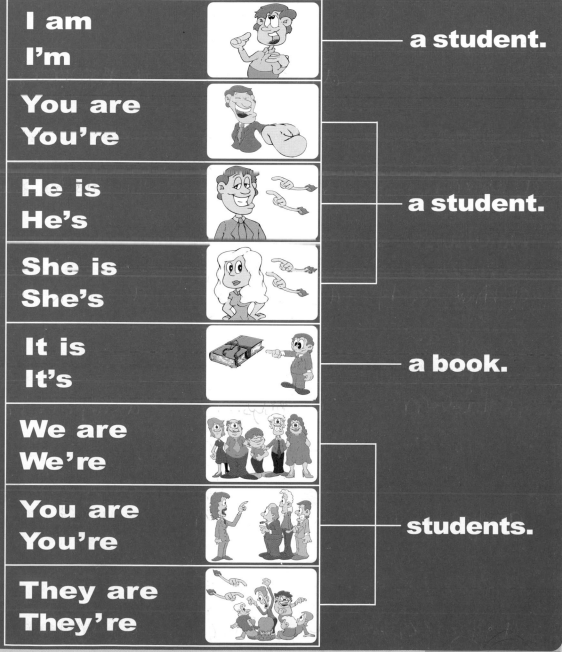

I am / I'm		a student.
You are / You're		
He is / He's		a student.
She is / She's		
It is / It's		a book.
We are / We're		
You are / You're		students.
They are / They're		

Jobs
(Listen and repeat)

1. *a doctor*
2. a mechanic
3. a reporter
4. a Pharmacist
5. a waiter — bosboy
6. a hair dresser
7. a Disc Jockey
8. a Construction worker
9. a cook-Chef
10. a lawyer
11. a babysitter
12. a Carpenter's
13. a dentist
14. a mailcarrier — Postman
15. a waitress — waiter
16. a Plumber
17. a waiter
18. a Cashier

ZONI ENGLISH SYSTEM ©

A: I'm a teacher.
Are you a teacher?

B: Yes, I'm a teacher.
Yes, I am.

Interaction

Pair Practice

Performance

A: I'm a construction worker.
Are you a construction worker?

B: Yes, I'm a construction worker.
Yes, I am.

(Entire class participation)

Imagination

(Listen and repeat)

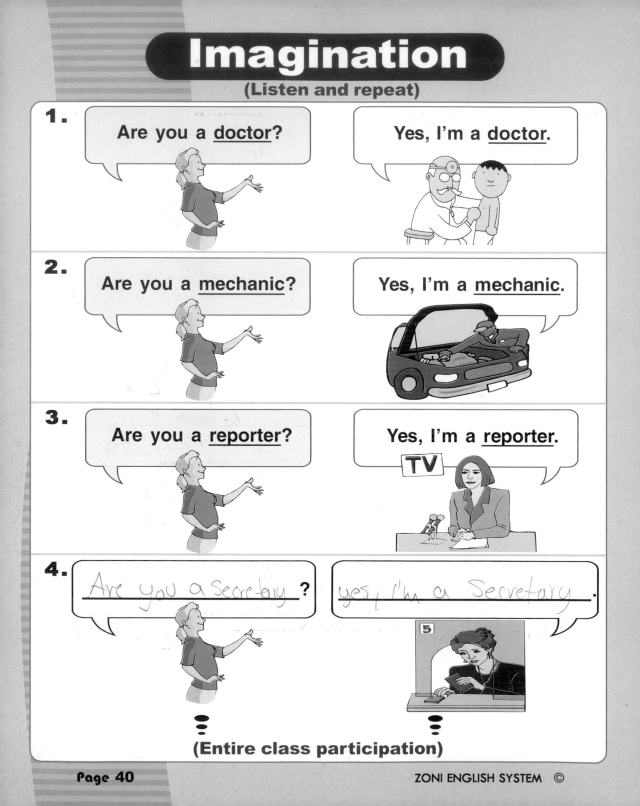

1. Are you a <u>doctor</u>? Yes, I'm a <u>doctor</u>.

2. Are you a <u>mechanic</u>? Yes, I'm a <u>mechanic</u>.

3. Are you a <u>reporter</u>? Yes, I'm a <u>reporter</u>.

4. Are you a Secretary? yes, I'm a Secretary.

(Entire class participation)

ZONI ENGLISH SYSTEM ©

Vocabulary-*Adjectives*

shy *Timido*   confused *confuso*   sick *enfermo*   smart *listo*   hungry *hambriento*
tired *cansado*   busy *atareado*   romantic   friendly *amistoso*   happy *Feliz*
crazy *loco*   angry *enojado*   cold *Frio*   thirsty *sediento*   sad *triste*

Chul Soo
Tony
Bertha
Jona
ceylainy
<u>h a p p y</u>

Richard
<u>t h i r s t y</u>

Ying
<u>F r i e n d l y</u>

George
<u>s a d</u>

Ahmet
Angry
<u>c o l d</u>

Nancy
<u>s h y</u>

Miguel
<u>t i r e d</u>

Freddy
Alfredo
<u>c r a z y</u>

Tony
exam 100%
<u>s m a r t</u>

Ann
<u>b u s y</u>

Keith
Alfredo
<u>r o m a n t i c</u>

Frank
<u>c o n f u s e d</u>

John
<u>h u n g r y</u>

Peter
<u>a n g r y</u>

Henry
<u>s i c k</u>

ZONI ENGLISH SYSTEM ©

Oral Practice
He is / She is
(Listen and repeat)

1. Is Chul Soo angry or happy?　　He is happy.

2. Is Ann tired or busy?　　She is busy.

3. Is George happy or sad?　　He is sad.

4. Is John thirsty or hungry?　　He is hungry.

5. Is Freddy crazy or angry?　　He is crazy.

Oral Practice

Is he hungry?	**No, he's not hungry.** **No, he's not.**
Is she shy?	**No, she's not shy.** **No, she's not.**

(Listen and repeat)

1.

Is Miguel hungry?

No, he's not hungry. He's tired.

2.

Is Ying shy?

No, she's not shy. She's friendly.

3.

Is George happy?

No, *He's not happy He's sad*.

4. Is Tony confused?

No, _He's not confused_. _He's smart_.

5. Is Peter happy?

No, _He's not happy_. _He's angry_.

6. Is Richard hungry?

No, _He's not hungry_. _He's thirsty_.

7. Is Keith shy?

No, _He's not shy_. _He's romantic_.

8. Is Ahmet thirsty?

No, _He's not thirsty_. _He is cold_.

9. Is Nancy sad?

No, _She's not sad_. _She's shy_.

Oral Practice

Change to questions.

1. He's a baseball player.

Is he a baseball player?

2. He's angry.

Is he angry ?

3. She's young.

Is she young ?

4. He's old.

Is He old ?

5. He's a politician.

Vote for me

Is He a politician ?

6. She's a tennis player.

Is she a tennis player?

7. He's a mechanic.

Is He a mechanic ?

8. She's a tutor.

Is she a tutor ?

Interaction

Where are you from?

I'm from the United States.

How old are you?

I'm 25 years old.

Are you married?

Yes, I'm married.

Age: 25

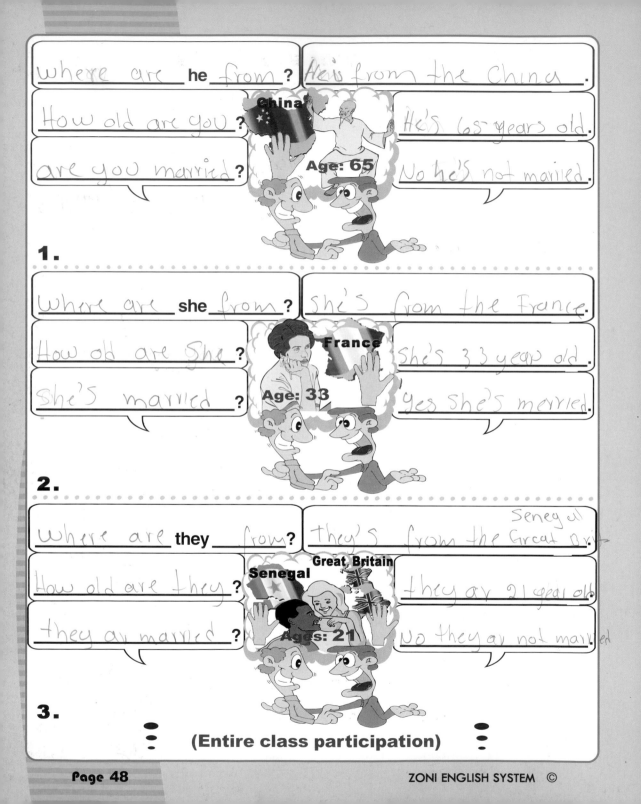

where are **he** from ? He is from the China .

How old are you ? He's 65 years old .

are you married ? No he's not married .

China

Age: 65

1.

where are **she** from ? she's from the France .

How old are She ? she's 3 3 year old .

she's married ? Yes she's married .

France

Age: 33

2.

where are **they** from? they's from the Great Brit Senegal

How old are they ? they ar 21 year old

they ar married ? No they ar not married

Senegal

Great Britain

Ages: 21

3.

(Entire class participation)

How's the weather? It's ...

(Listen and repeat)

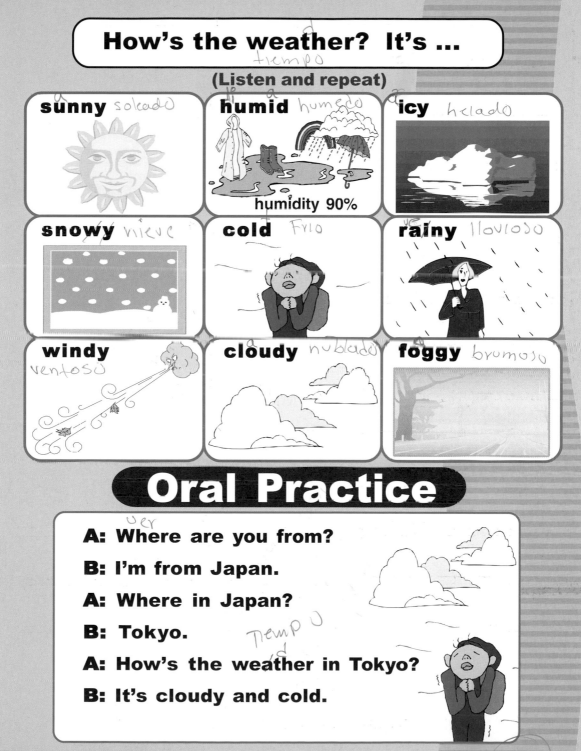

sunny solsado

humid humedo

humidity 90%

icy helado

snowy nieve

cold Frio

rainy llovioso

windy ventoso

cloudy nublado

foggy brumoso

Oral Practice

A: Where are you from?

B: I'm from Japan.

A: Where in Japan?

B: Tokyo.

A: How's the weather in Tokyo?

B: It's cloudy and cold.

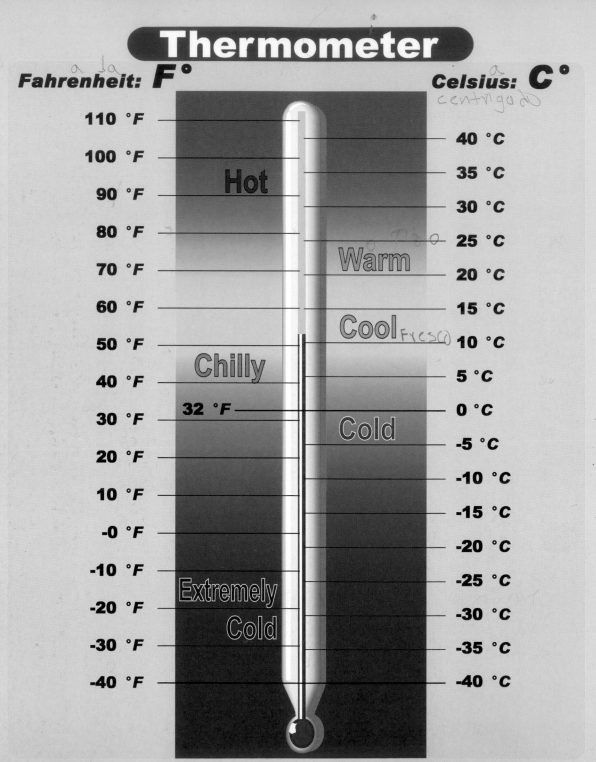

Thermometer

Fahrenheit: F°   **Celsius: C°**

Fahrenheit	Description	Celsius
110 °F		40 °C
100 °F	Hot	35 °C
90 °F		30 °C
80 °F		25 °C
70 °F	Warm	20 °C
60 °F		15 °C
50 °F	Cool	10 °C
40 °F	Chilly	5 °C
32 °F		0 °C
30 °F	Cold	-5 °C
20 °F		-10 °C
10 °F		-15 °C
-0 °F		-20 °C
-10 °F	Extremely Cold	-25 °C
-20 °F		-30 °C
-30 °F		-35 °C
-40 °F		-40 °C

Interaction

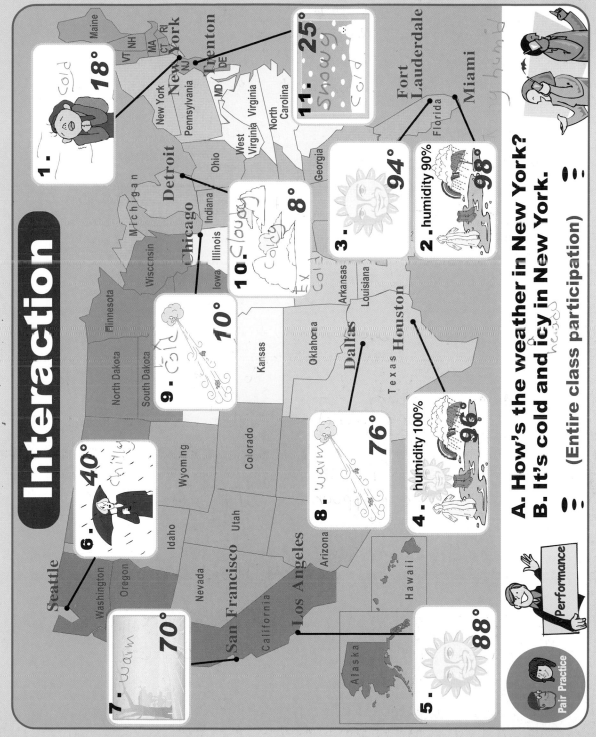

1. 18° Cold

11. 25° Snowy Cold

2. humidity 90% 98°

3. 94°

10. Cloudy Tex Cold 8°

9. Cold 10°

8. Warm 76°

6. Chilly 40°

4. humidity 100% 96°

7. Warm 70°

5. 88°

A. How's the weather in New York?
B. It's cold and icy in New York.

= = (Entire class participation) = =

Performance

Pair Practice

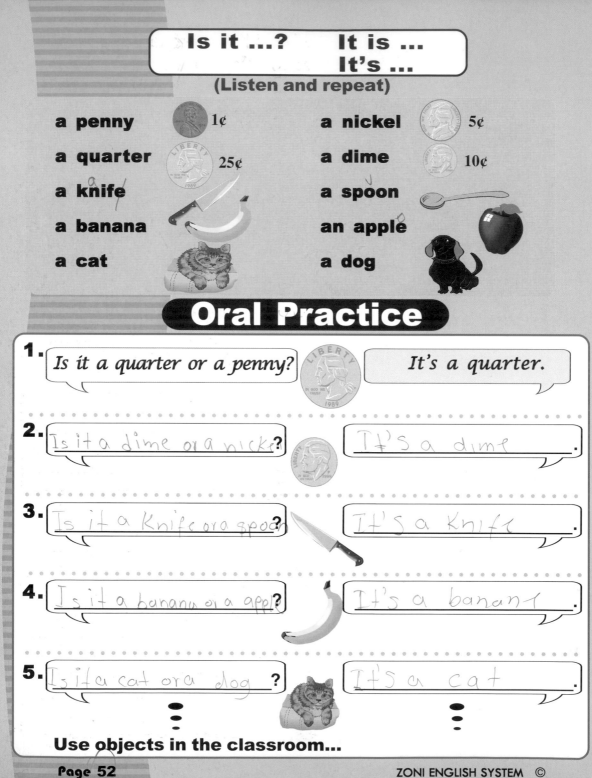

Is it ...?   It is ...
It's ...
(Listen and repeat)

a penny	1¢	a nickel	5¢
a quarter	25¢	a dime	10¢
a knife		a spoon	
a banana		an apple	
a cat		a dog	

Oral Practice

1. Is it a quarter or a penny?   It's a quarter.

2. Is it a dime or a nickel?   It's a dime.

3. Is it a knife or a spoon?   It's a knife.

4. Is it a banana or a apple?   It's a banana.

5. Is it a cat or a dog?   It's a cat.

Use objects in the classroom...

Is it a pen? No, it's not a pen. No, it's not.

(Listen and repeat)

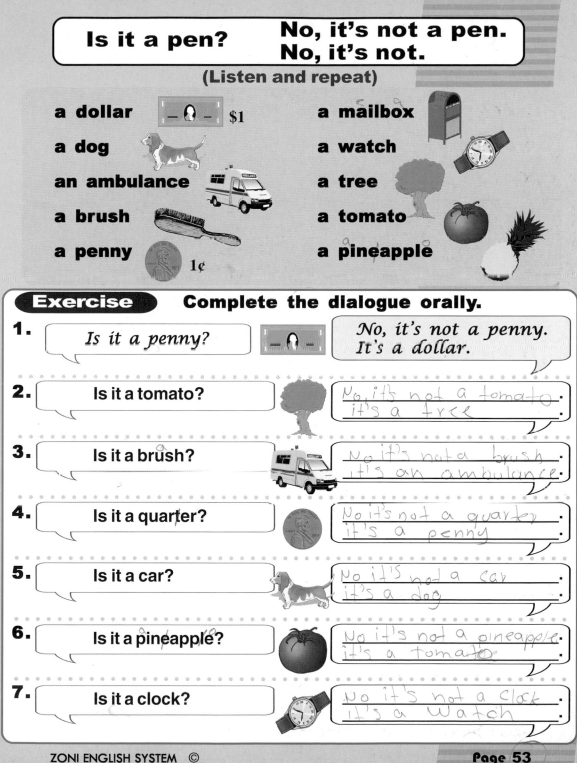

a dollar $1

a dog

an ambulance

a brush

a penny   1¢

a mailbox

a watch

a tree

a tomato

a pineapple

Exercise   Complete the dialogue orally.

1. Is it a penny? — No, it's not a penny. It's a dollar.

2. Is it a tomato? — No, it's not a tomato. it's a tree.

3. Is it a brush? — No it's not a brush. it's an ambulance.

4. Is it a quarter? — No it's not a quarter. it's a penny

5. Is it a car? — No it's not a car. it's a dog

6. Is it a pineapple? — No it's not a pineapple. it's a tomato

7. Is it a clock? — No it's not a clock. it's a watch

ZONI ENGLISH SYSTEM ©   Page 53

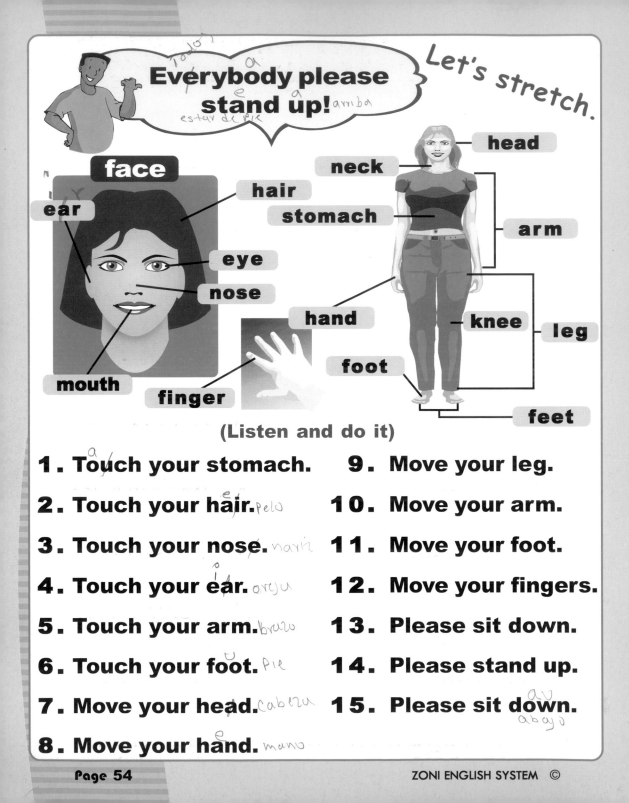

Everybody please stand up!

Let's stretch.

face

ear · hair · eye · nose · mouth · finger · stomach · hand · foot

head · neck · arm · knee · leg · feet

(Listen and do it)

1. Touch your stomach.
2. Touch your hair.
3. Touch your nose.
4. Touch your ear.
5. Touch your arm.
6. Touch your foot.
7. Move your head.
8. Move your hand.
9. Move your leg.
10. Move your arm.
11. Move your foot.
12. Move your fingers.
13. Please sit down.
14. Please stand up.
15. Please sit down.

ZONI ENGLISH SYSTEM ©

1. _____

2. _____

3. _____

4. _____

5. _____

6. _____

7. _____

8. _____

9. _____

10. _____

deberes

Homework 1

Exercise A   **Write the personal pronoun in the blanks.**

1. Peter is happy.   _He_ is happy.
2. Mary is sad.   _She_ is sad.
3. Lisa and Michael are home. (hogar)   _They_ are home.
4. The book is red.   _It_ is red.
5. The pens (pluma) are cheap. (barato)   _It_ are cheap.
6. Nancy and I are related. (relacionado)   _We_ are related.
7. Susan is from Spain.   _She_ is from Spain.
8. Robert is a teacher.   _He_ is a teacher.
9. Robert and I are teachers.   _We_ are teachers.
10. Coffee is cheap. (barato)   _It_ is cheap.

Exercise B   **Write the verb _to be_ in the blanks.**

1. They _are_ my friends.
2. She _is_ sick. (enfermo)
3. We _are_ late for work.
4. It _is_ expensive. (caro)
5. Mohammed _is_ short.
6. You _are_ a student.
7. You _are_ students.
8. My teacher _is_ good.
9. I _am_ hungry. (hambriento)
10. It _is_ hot today.
11. Pat _is_ my teacher.
12. We _are_ busy. (atareado)
13. They _are_ married.
14. I _am_ single. (soltera)
15. English _is_ easy. (Fácil)
16. Hakan _is_ happy.
17. He _is_ tall. (alto)
18. They _are_ sad. (triste)
19. It _is_ a car.
20. John _is_ smart. (listo)

ZONI ENGLISH SYSTEM ©

Exercise C — Change to contractions.

1. She is a nurse.   _She's a nurse._ enfermera
2. He is a doctor.   He's a doctor
3. They are lawyers.   They're lawyers abogados
4. We are mechanics.   We're mechanics
5. It is a chair.   it's a chair
6. I am hungry.   I'm hungry hambriento
7. She is busy.   She's busy atareada
8. He is a dentist.   He's a dentist
9. They are students.   They're students
10. It is blue.   It's blue

Exercise D — Change to the negative.

1. He is a carpenter.

   He's not a carpenter.

2. They are from Venezuela.

   They'ar not from Venezuela

3. I am twenty years old.

   I'm not twenty years old

4. We are hungry.

   We'ar not hungry

5. She is in the hospital.

   She's not in the hospital

6. It is a car.

   It's not a car

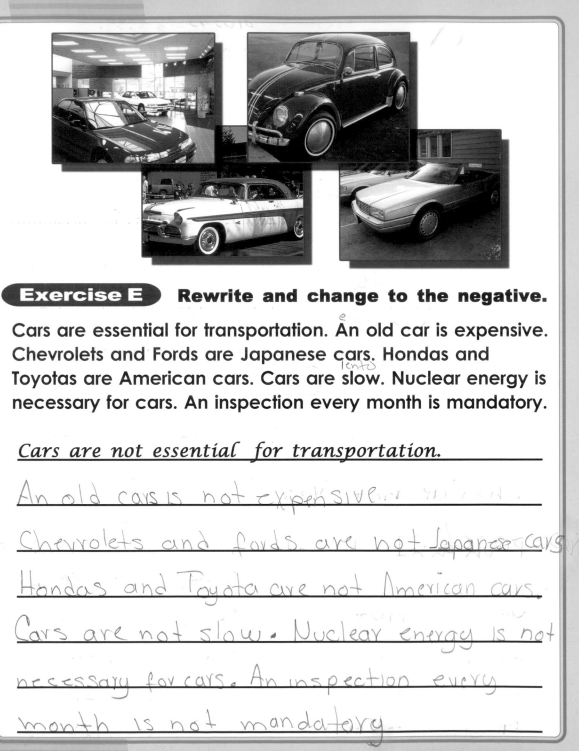

Exercise E   **Rewrite and change to the negative.**

Cars are essential for transportation. An old car is expensive. Chevrolets and Fords are Japanese cars. Hondas and Toyotas are American cars. Cars are slow. Nuclear energy is necessary for cars. An inspection every month is mandatory.

Cars are not essential for transportation.

An old cars is not expensive.

Chevrolets and fords are not Japanese cars.

Hondas and Toyota are not American cars.

Cars are not slow. Nuclear energy is not

necessary for cars. An inspection every

month is not mandatory.

Homework 2

Change to the negative.

1. **Linda is happy.**
Linda is not happy

2. **Mohammed is sad.**
Mohammed is not sad

3. **Nelly and Mary are overweight.** _demaciado gordo_
Nelly and Mary are not overweight

4. **The cake is delicious.**
The cake is not delicious

5. **The books are good.**
The books are not good

6. **Jimmy and I are hungry.**
Jimmy and I are not hungry

7. **Anthony is from Italy.**
Anthony is not from Italy

8. **Berfin is a teacher.**
Berfin is not a teacher

9. **Maria and I are students.**
Maria and I are not students

10. **Diamonds are beautiful.**
Diamonds are not beautiful

Exercise B   **Write the negative of the verb _to be_.**

1. They _ar not_ my friends.

2. She _'s not_ a teacher.

3. We _ar not_ tall.

4. Ann _'s not_ short.

5. You _ar not_ a student.

6. He _'s not_ intelligent.

7. I _'m not_ single. _soltero_

8. It _'s not_ hot.

9. John _'s not_ in school.

10. She _'s not_ thirsty. _sediento_

Exercise C   Circle the correct answer. respuesta

1. He ___IS___ a doorman. portero
   A: (is)   B: are   C: am

2. They ___are___ in California.
   A: is   B: (are)   C: am

3. Are ___you___ the teacher?
   A: (you)   B: they   C: I

4. Is ___she___ from Colombia?
   A: you   B: we   C: (she)

5. I ___am___ a pilot.
   A: is   B: (am)   C: are

6. She ___IS___ a nurse. enfermera
   A: (is)   B: are   C: am

7. You ___are___ police officers.
   A: is   B: am   C: (are)

8. Are ___you___ students?
   A: (you)   B: she   C: he

9. ___are___ they children?
   A: Is   B: (Are)   C: We

10. ___IS___ he young?
    A: (Is)   B: Are   C: Am

Exercise D — Write the correct article *A* or *An*.

1. _An_ apple
2. _A_ house
3. _A_ chair
4. _A_ book
5. _An_ orange

6. _A_ student
7. _An_ island
8. _An_ egg *huevo*
9. _A_ notebook *cuaderno*
10. _An_ umbrella

Exercise E — Write the correct pronoun.

1. The book is new. ___It___ is new.

2. Susan and Yuki are friends. ___They___ are friends.

3. John is a driver. ___He___ is a driver.

4. The cat is hungry. ___It___ is hungry.

5. Hakan and I are busy. ___We___ are busy.

6. Lisa is happy. ___She___ is happy.

7. The cars are in the garage. ___they___ are in the garage.

8. You and Mary are single. ___you___ are single.

9. Mr. Peng is a lawyer. ___He___ is a lawyer.

10. Mrs. Smith is a doctor. ___She___ is a doctor.

Summary

AFFIRMATIVE	AFFIRMATIVE CONTRACTION
I *am*	I'*m*
You *are*	You'*re*
He *is*	He'*s*
She *is* happy.	She'*s* happy.
It *is*	It'*s*
We *are*	We'*re*
You *are*	You'*re*
They *are*	They'*re*

NEGATIVE	NEGATIVE CONTRACTION
I *am not*	I'*m not*
You *are not*	You'*re not*
He *is not*	He'*s not*
She *is not* happy.	She'*s not* happy.
It *is not*	It'*s not*
We *are not*	We'*re not*
You *are not*	You'*re not*
They *are not*	They'*re not*

QUESTIONS

Am I
Are you
Is he
Is she   happy?
Is it
Are we
Are you
Are they

Lesson 3

What's that?

This/That

Nouns

These/Those

Vocabulary
(Listen and repeat)

1. television

2. board

3. chair

4. eraser

5. watch

6. clock

7. door

8. desk

9. pencil

10. umbrella

11. window

12. notebook

Oral Practice
What is a...?

Demonstrate with the objects in the classroom.

1.

What is a clock?

This is a clock.

That is a clock.

2. board
3. notebook
4. eraser

5. shirt
6. bag
7. door

8. television
9. desk
10. watch

(Entire class participation)

ZONI ENGLISH SYSTEM ©

This / That
SINGULAR
(Listen and repeat)

What's this?

This is a candle.

What's that?

That is a chair.

Exercise

Answer the questions. Use *this is* or *that is*.

1. What's this?

This is a cap.

cap

2. What's that?

That is a shirt.

shirt

3. What's that?

That is a Church.

church

4. What's this?

This is a carrot.

carrot

Oral Practice

1.

| What's this? | 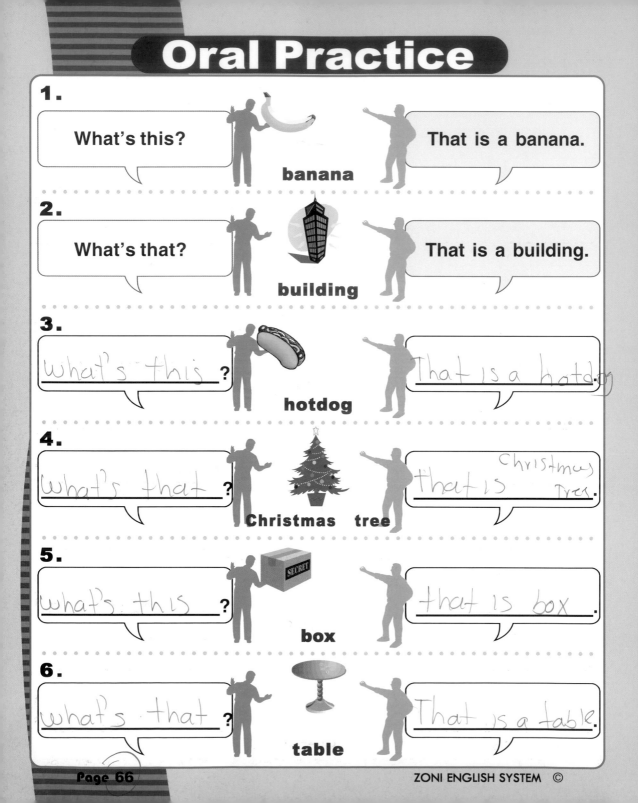 | That is a banana. |

banana

2.

What's that?

building

That is a building.

3.

What's this ?

hotdog

That is a hotdog

4.

what's that ?

Christmas tree

that is Christmas Tree.

5.

what's this ?

box

that is box.

6.

what's that ?

table

That is a table.

7.

What's that?

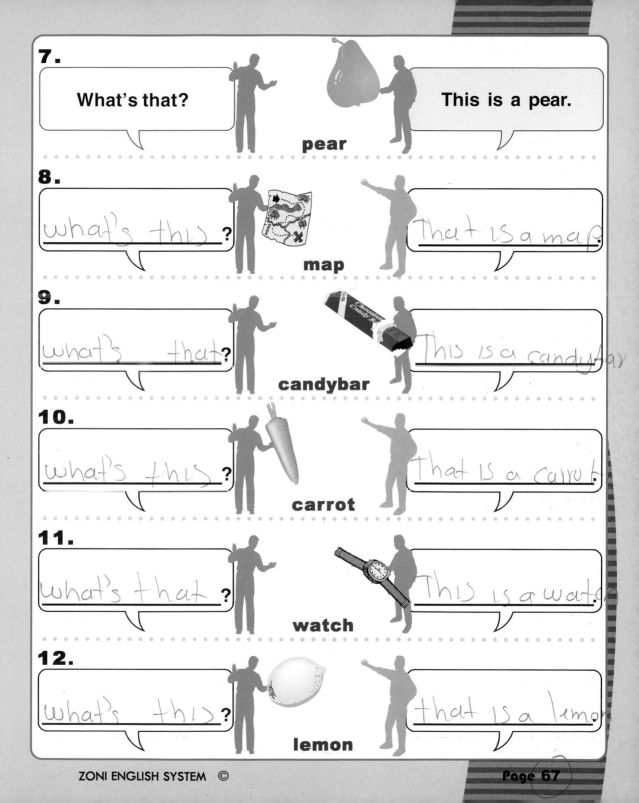

pear

This is a pear.

8.

what's this?

map

That is a map.

9.

what's that?

candybar

This is a candybar

10.

what's this?

carrot

that is a carrot.

11.

what's that?

watch

This is a watch.

12.

what's this?

lemon

that is a lemon

This is not / That is not
Oral Practice

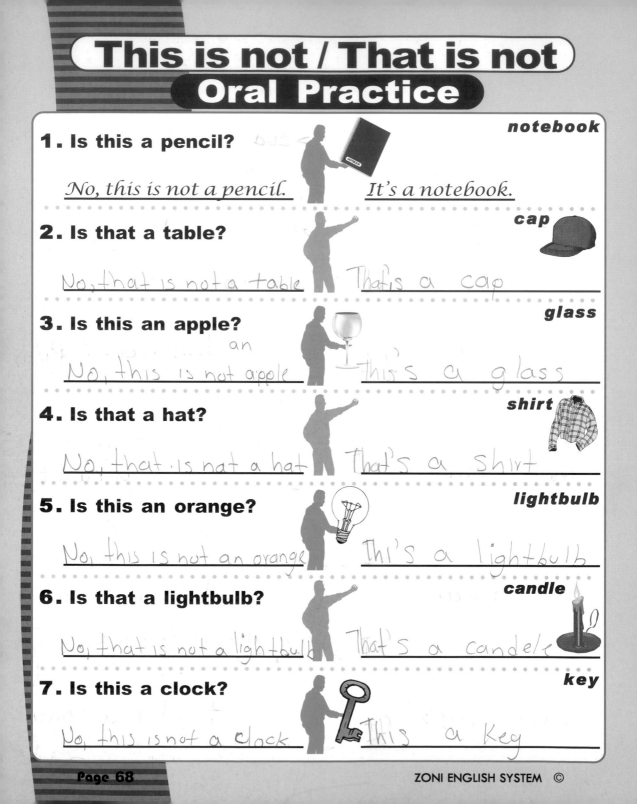

1. **Is this a pencil?**
notebook

<u>*No, this is not a pencil.*</u>   *It's a notebook.*

2. **Is that a table?**
cap

No, that is not a table   That's a cap

3. **Is this an apple?**
glass

an
No, this is not apple   this's a glass

4. **Is that a hat?**
shirt

No, that is not a hat   That's a shirt

5. **Is this an orange?**
lightbulb

No, this is not an orange   Thi's a lightbulb

6. **Is that a lightbulb?**
candle

No, that is not a lightbulb   That's a candele

7. **Is this a clock?**
key

No, this is not a clock   This a Key

ZONI ENGLISH SYSTEM ©

Nouns
A noun is a person, place or thing.
(Listen and repeat)

(handwritten annotations: sustantivo, a, cosa, escuchar)

Singular	Plural

car

cars

Use "es" when the last letter(s) of the noun is s, x, ch, sh or o.

(handwritten: usan, cuando, ultimo, sustantivo)

bus

bus*es*

box

box *es*

watch

watch *es*

brush

brush *es*

tomato

tomato *es*

Use "ies" when the noun ends in consonant + "y."

(handwritten: acaban)

fly

fl*ies*

Change to the plural.

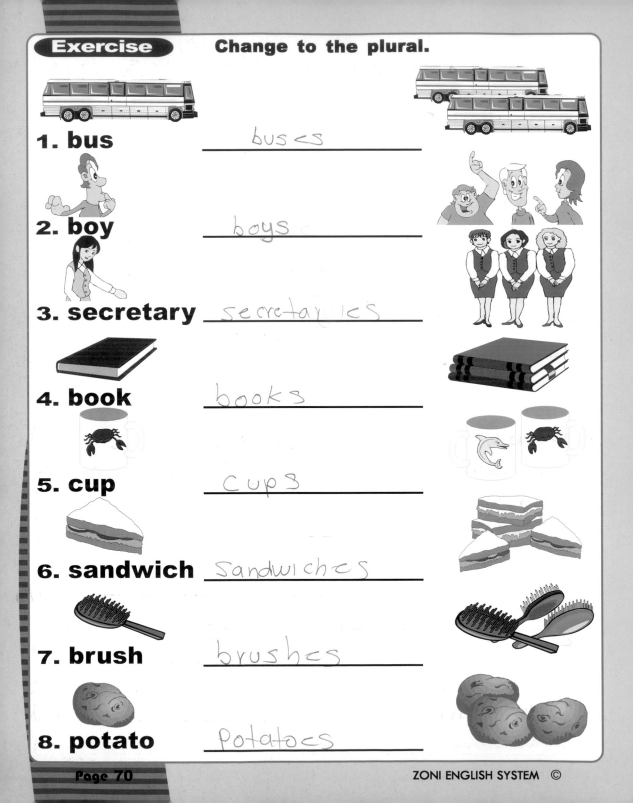

1. bus _____buses_____

2. boy _____boys_____

3. secretary _____secretaries_____

4. book _____books_____

5. cup _____cups_____

6. sandwich _____sandwiches_____

7. brush _____brushes_____

8. potato _____potatoes_____

Homework

Change to the plural.

Singular	Plural
1. door	doors
2. orange	oranges
3. box	boxes
4. church	churches
5. secretary	secretaries
6. egg	eggs
7. boy	boys
8. lady	ladies
9. dish	dishes
10. exercise	exercises
11. eraser	erasers
12. glass	glasses
13. party	parties
14. airplane	airplanes
15. automobile	automobiles
16. train	trains
17. building	buildings

Irregulars

Singular	Plural
1. man	men
2. woman	women
3. person	people
4. child	children

These / Those
PLURAL
(Listen and repeat)

What are these?

These are watches.

What are those?

Those are newspapers.

Exercise

Answer the questions. Use *these are* or *those are*.

1. What are these?

These are matches.

matches

2. What are those?

Those are cats

cats

3. What are those?

Those are radios

radios

4. What are these?

These are clocks

clocks

ZONI ENGLISH SYSTEM ©

Oral Practice

1.

What are these? — hats — Those are hats.

2.

What are those? — televisions — Those are televisions.

3.

what are these? — keys — Those are Keys.

4.

what are those? — socks — Those are socks.

5.

what are these? — pills — Those are pills.

6.

what are those? — muffins — Those are muffins

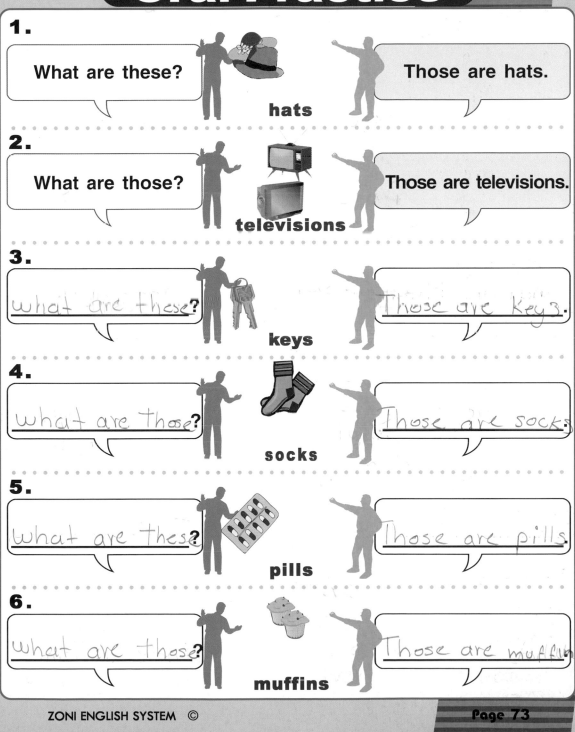

7.

What are those?

glasses

These are glasses.

8.

What are these?

grapes

Those are grapes.

9.

What are those?

watches

These are watches.

10.

What are these?

lightbulbs

Those are lightbulbs
lightbulbs

11.

What are those?

candles

These are candles.

12.

What are these?

lemons

Those are lemons.

Homework

Write sentences. Use _this_, _that_, _these_ or _those_.

1. _This is a desk._

2. Those are dogs

3. This is a car

4. These are a bananas

5. That is a mailbox

6. These are pens

7. Those are chairs

8. This is a book

SINGULAR	PLURAL
This	These
That	Those

Oral Practice
(Listen and repeat)

Change to questions.

1. This is a pencil.

Is this a pencil?

2. These are pencils.

are these pencils ?

3. This is a chair.

Is this a chair ?

4. These are chairs.

are these chairs ?

5. That is a bag.

Is that a bag ?

6. Those are bags.

are those bag ?

7. That is a washing machine.

Is that a washing machin?

8. Those are washing machines.

are those washing machin?

These are not / Those are not
Oral Practice
(Listen and repeat)

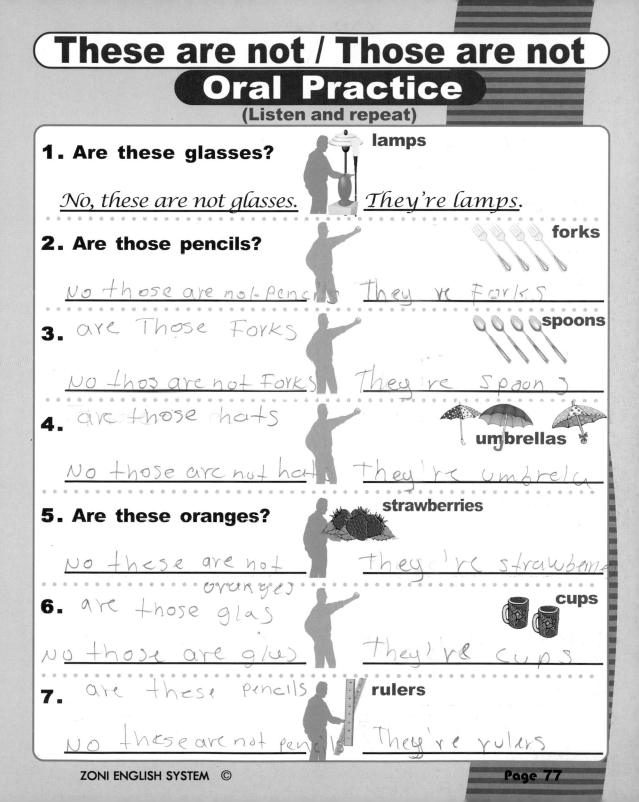

1. Are these glasses?   lamps

No, these are not glasses.   *They're lamps.*

2. Are those pencils?   forks

No those are not Pencils They're Forks

3. are Those Forks   spoons

No thos are not Forks They're spoons

4. are those hats   umbrellas

No those are not hats They're umbrela

5. Are these oranges?   strawberries

No these are not   They're strawbern
oranges

6. are those glas   cups

No those are glas They're cups

7. are these pencils   rulers

No these are not pencils They're rulers

1. That is a frien Frame

2. Those are my friens Frends

Pairs
3. These are pers of shoos

4. This is his cap of cofee

5. are these your books?

Homework

Exercise A — Write *is* or *are* in the blank.

1. This ___is___ a table.
2. These ___are___ tables.
3. That ___is___ a door.
4. Those ___are___ doors.
5. This ___is___ a window.

6. These ___are___ windows.
7. That ___is___ a dictionary.
8. Those ___are___ dictionaries.
9. Those ___are___ pens.
10. These ___are___ apples.

Exercise B — Change to the plural.

Singular	Plural
1. This is a lamp.	These are lamps
2. That is a car.	Those are cars
3. This is a book.	These are books
4. That is a toy.	Those are toys
5. This is a dish.	These are dishes
6. That is a fly.	Those are flies
7. This is an apple.	These are apples
8. That is a box.	Those are boxes
9. That is a board.	Those are boards
10. That is a key.	Those are keys

Practice writing the following words.

a chair	a clock	an eraser	an umbrella
a chair	a clock	an eraser	an umbrella
a chair	a clock	an erasey	an umbrella
a chair	a clock	an erasey	an umbrella
a chair	a clock	an erasey	an umbrella
a chair	a clock	an erasey	an umbrella
a chair	a clock	an erasey	an umbrella
a chair	a clock	an erasey	an umbrella

a box	a cup	a key	a shirt
a box	a cup	a key	a shirt
a box	a cup	a key	a shirt
a box	a cup	a key	a shirt
a box	a cup	a key	a shirt
a box	a cup	a key	a shirt
a box	a cap	a key	a shirt
a box	a cap	a key	a shirt

ZONI ENGLISH SYSTEM ©

Exercise D

Match the vocabulary with the correct picture.

1. this chair _____E_____

2. that chair _____H_____

3. a watch _____F_____

4. a clock _____J_____

5. a toy _____B_____

6. an umbrella _____D_____

7. a window _____C_____

8. an eraser _____I_____

9. a notebook _____G_____

10. an apple _____A_____

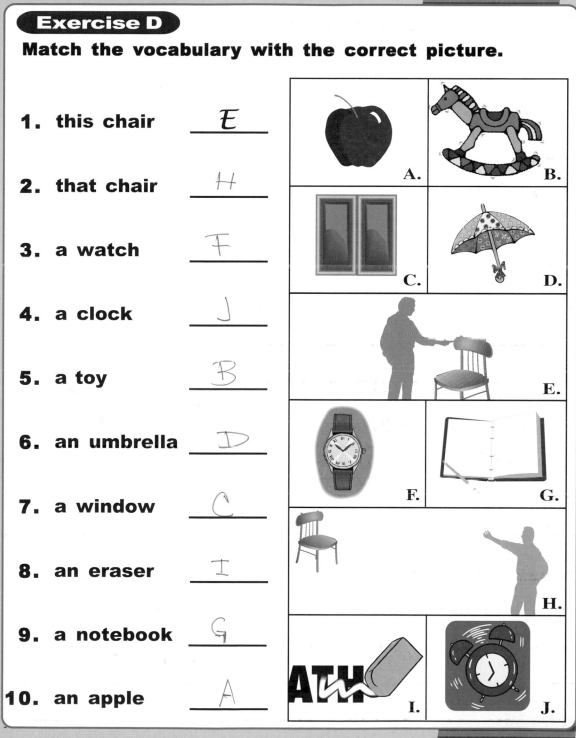

A. B. C. D. E. F. G. H. I. J.

Summary
Demonstrative Adjectives

		SINGULAR	PLURAL
Near *cerca*	**Affirmative**	This is	These are
Far *(lejos)*		That is **That's** *CONTRACTION*	Those are
Near	**Negative**	This is not	These are not
Far		That is not **That's not** *CONTRACTION*	Those are not
Near	**Question**	Is this ...? *Answer* Responder Yes, it is. No, it is not.	Are these ...? *Answer* Yes, they are. No, they are not.
Far		Is that ...? *Answer* Yes, it is. No, it is not.	Are those ...? *Answer* Yes, they are. No, they are not.

Article	No Article
<u>a</u> book	book<u>s</u>
<u>an</u> orange	orange<u>s</u>

ZONI ENGLISH SYSTEM ©

lesson 4

I'm sorry I'm late.

Time
Time Expressions

What time is it?
(Listen and repeat)

ZONI ENGLISH SYSTEM ©

4.

Hello.

It's _Fifteen minutes to Five._

`4:45`

5.

Good morning.

It's _Ten minutes to seven._

`9:35`

6.

It's _eleven o five_.

`11:05`

Oral Practice
(Listen and repeat)

Morning	AM
Afternoon Evening Night	PM

1. What time is it?

2:00 ● PM AM

It's two o'clock.

2. What time is it?

5:00 ● PM AM

It's Five o' clock

3. What time is it?

7:00 ● PM AM

it's seven o' clock

4. What time is it?

9:00 ● PM AM

it's nine o' clock

Homework

What time is it?

1. <u>nine o'clock</u>

2. <u>six thirty</u>

3. <u>Five minutes to Three</u>

4. <u>eight Twentyfive</u>

5. <u>Five a clock</u>

6. <u>Twelve o'clock</u>

7. <u>Ten thirty five</u>

8. <u>Three Fifteen</u>

9. <u>Twelve thirty</u>

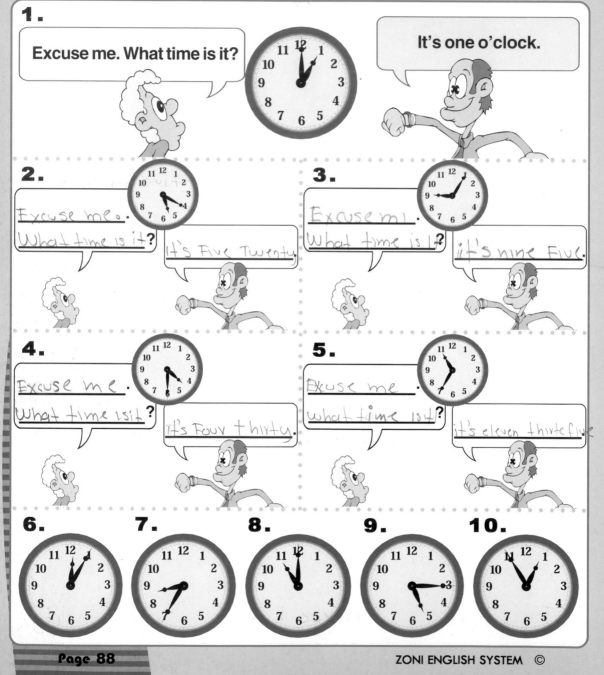

1.

Excuse me. What time is it?

It's one o'clock.

2.

Excuse me. What time is it?

It's Five Twenty.

3.

Excuse me. What time is it?

it's nine Five.

4.

Excuse me. What time is it?

It's Four thirty.

5.

Excuse me. What time is it?

it's eleven thirtefive

6. **7.** **8.** **9.** **10.**

ZONI ENGLISH SYSTEM ©

Everybody do it!

(handwritten: Todos)

(Listen and do it)

Everybody stand up!
Clap 10 times!
Turn around! *(handwritten: girar alrededor)*
Stretch!
Raise your hands! *(handwritten: levantar)*
Sit down!
Everybody stand up!
Turn to the left! *(handwritten: izquierda)*
Turn to the right! *(handwritten: derecha)*
Sit down!

Homework

Exercise A Practice writing the following sentences.

1. I'm early. *Temprano*

2. I'm on time. *Sobre a Tiempo*

3. I'm late.

I'm early.	*I'm on time*	*I'm late*
I'm early.	*I'm on time*	*I'm late*
I'm early	I'm on time	I'm late
I'm early	I'm on time	I'm late
I'm early	I'm on time	I'm late
I'm early	I'm on time	I'm late
I'm early	I'm on time	I'm late

Exercise B Practice writing the following numbers.

13 thirteen	**3** three	**12** twelve	**30** thirty
thirteen	Three	Twelve	Thirty
thirteen	Three	Twelve	Thirty
Thirteen	Three	Twelve	Thirty
Thirteen	Three	Twelve	Thirty
Thirteen	Three	Twelve	Thirty
Thirteen	Three	Twelve	Thirty
Thirteen	Three	Twelve	Thirty

15 fifteen	**8** eight	**24** twenty-four	**11** eleven
Fifteen	eight	Twenty-four	eleven
Fifteen	eight	Twenty-four	eleven
Fifteen	eight	Twenty-four	eleven
Fifteen	eight	Twenty-four	eleven
Fifteen	eight	Twenty-four	eleven
Fifteen	eight	Twenty-four	eleven
Fifteen	eight	Twenty-four	eleven

Pronunciation Practice

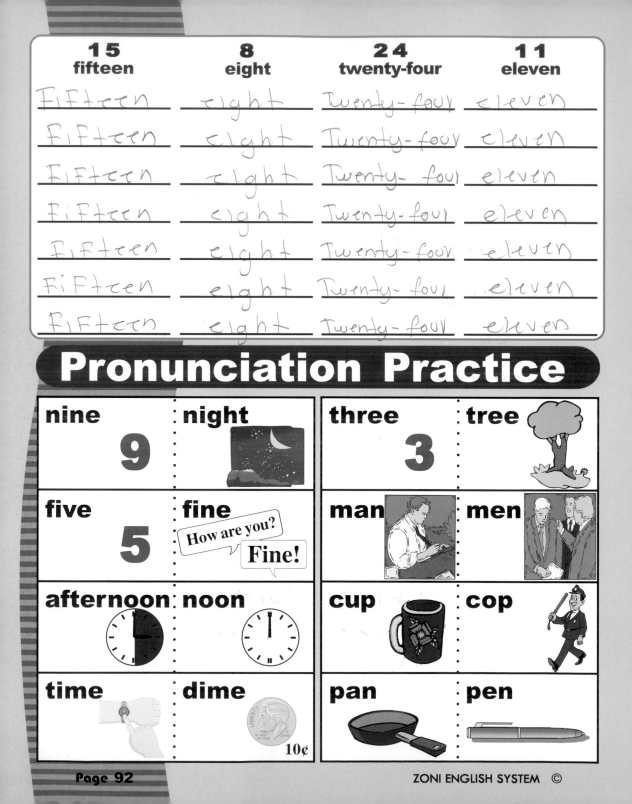

nine	night	three	tree
9		**3**	
five	fine	man	men
5	How are you? Fine!		
afternoon	noon	cup	cop
time	dime	pan	pen
	10¢		

ZONI ENGLISH SYSTEM ©

Whose
Possessive Nouns
Possessive Adjectives
Family

Whose
(Listen and repeat)

1.

Whose shirt is this?

Here you are.

You're welcome.

That's my shirt.

Thanks.

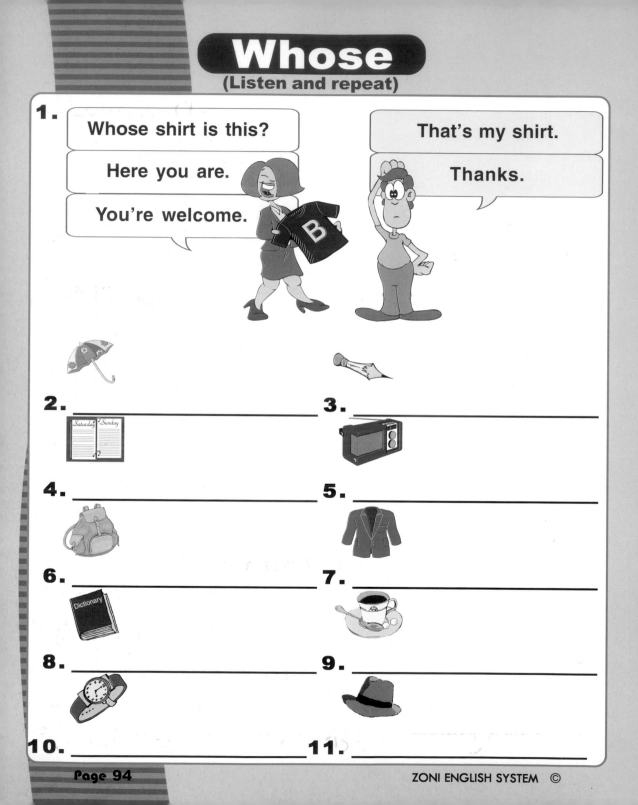

2. _____

3. _____

4. _____

5. _____

6. _____

7. _____

8. _____

9. _____

10. _____

11. _____

Personal Pronouns	Possessive Adjectives
I	My
You	Your
He	His
She	Her
It	Its
We	Our
You	Your
They	Their

Oral Practice

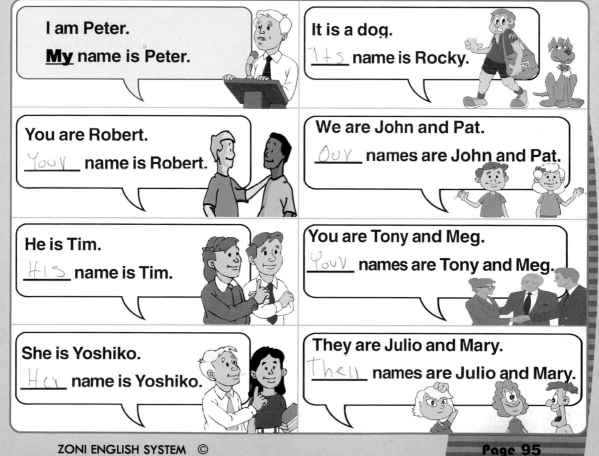

I am Peter.
My name is Peter.

It is a dog.
<u>Its</u> name is Rocky.

You are Robert.
<u>Your</u> name is Robert.

We are John and Pat.
<u>Our</u> names are John and Pat.

He is Tim.
<u>His</u> name is Tim.

You are Tony and Meg.
<u>Your</u> names are Tony and Meg.

She is Yoshiko.
<u>Her</u> name is Yoshiko.

They are Julio and Mary.
<u>Their</u> names are Julio and Mary.

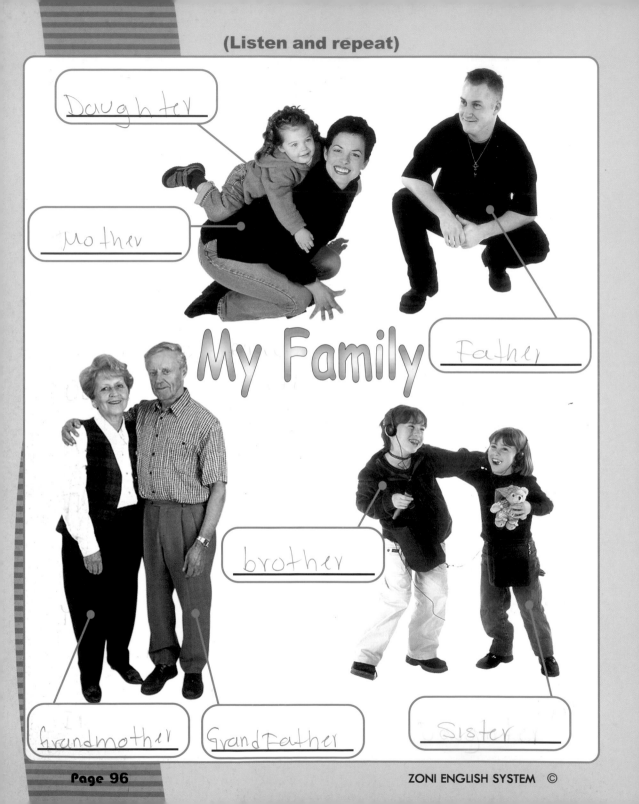

Daughter

Mother

Father

My Family

Grandmother

Grandfather

brother

Sister

This is My Family
(Listen and repeat)

My family is small.

There are 5 people in my family.

These are my parents.

Their names are Susan and Bill.

This is my sister.

Her name is Mary.

This is my brother.

His name is Billy.

My Family

Put your photograph here, or draw a picture of your family.
Talk about your family with your partner.

My family is great. There are 14
pipole in my family. Their name are
(This are) my sisters. Her name are
Juana, Oliveria, Cristina en Hermelinda
This are my brothers his name
are Raul, Guillermo, Arturo
Osvaldo, Juan Edgardo, Erain cy
Luis, My Father is Guillermo
My Mother is Lucy
My famill is Happy Happy

Homework

Exercise A   Write the correct possessive adjectives.

1. He is my brother. _His_ name is John.

2. She is my sister. _Her_ name is Cindy.

3. We are cousins. _Primo_

   Our names are Susan and David.

4. They are football players.

   Their names are David and Michael.

5. You are my teacher.

   Your name is Cristina.

6. The United States is a country.

   Its capital is Washington, D.C.

New York
Washington D.C.

ZONI ENGLISH SYSTEM ©

Write the correct possessive adjectives and change to the negative.

1. He is my brother.

___His___ name is _not_ Peter.

John

2. She is my sister.

___Her___ name is _not_ Ann.

Cindy

3. We are cousins.

___Our___ names are _not_ Diana and John.

Susan and David

4. They are football players.

___Their___ names are _not_ Tony and Fred.

David and Michael

5. You are my teacher.

___Your___ name is _not_ Maya.

Cristina

6. The United States is a country.

___Its___ capital is _not_ New York.

New York
Washington D.C.

Possessive Nouns

noun's

1.

This is <u>Young Hee's</u> mother.

This is <u>her</u> mother.

Young Hee

2.

This is John's book.

This is <u>his</u> book.

John

3.

This is ___Luis'___ toy.

This is ___His___ toy.

Luis

4.

This is ___Kathy's___ wallet.

This is ___Her___ wallet.

Kathy

Possessive Nouns
(Listen and repeat)

1.

This is <u>Rosana's</u> car.

<u>Rosana's</u> car is new.

Rosana

2.

This is <u>Christopher's</u> house.

<u>Christopher's</u> house is beautiful.

Christopher

3.

This is <u>Pamela's</u> sister.

<u>Pamela's</u> sister is a tennis player.

Pamela

4.

This is <u>Brian's</u> computer.

<u>Brian's</u> computer is old.

Brian

ZONI ENGLISH SYSTEM ©

Oral Practice

Use possessive nouns.

Nancy / horse

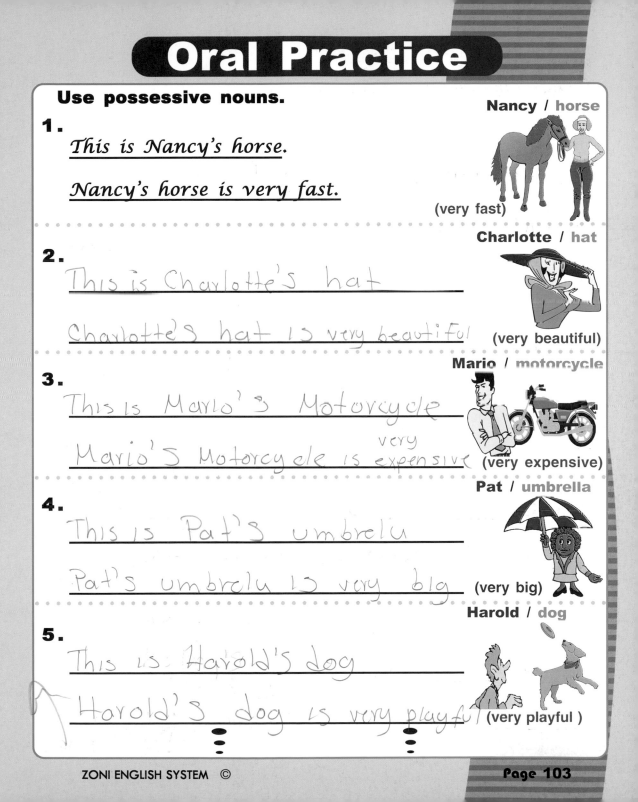

1.

This is Nancy's horse.

Nancy's horse is very fast.

(very fast)

Charlotte / hat

2.

This is Charlotte's hat

Charlotte's hat is very beautiful

(very beautiful)

Mario / motorcycle

3.

This is Mario's Motorcycle

Mario's Motorcycle is very expensive

(very expensive)

Pat / umbrella

4.

This is Pat's umbrelu

Pat's umbrelu is very big

(very big)

Harold / dog

5.

This is Harold's dog

Harold's dog is very playful

(very playful)

Oral Practice

1. Whose book is this? — That's Maria's book.

2. pen — Pablo

3. dictionary — John

4. cap — Nancy

5. dog — Diana

6. sharpener — Sandra

7. umbrella — Paul

8. calculator — Silvia

Use objects in the classroom.

ZONI ENGLISH SYSTEM ©

1. Whose capkel are   these ?.
        cupcakes

2. those are   yues and Jacks park Mex
              greg's   apurlimonts

3. these is your glases of wller
   Is This   class   water

4. No that's not   my cup of coffee
      it's John's

5. Ronald's car is bery   spencil
              very   expinslve

Homework

Exercise A   Change to questions. _Pregunta_

1. **This is his book.**

   Is this his book ?

2. **Those are my keys.**

   Are Those my keys ?

3. **He is your brother.**

   Is He your brother ?

4. **She is our teacher.**

   Is She our teacher ?

5. **It is their car.**

   Is It their car ?

6. **That is my wallet.**

   Is that my wallet ?

7. **Our father is at home.**

   Is Our father at home ?

8. **Their jackets are in her closet.**

   Are their Jackets in her closet ?

9. **Our food is on the table.**

   Is Our food on the table ?

10. **They are in my class.**

    Are they in my class ?

Use the correct possessive adjectives.

1. Ann is a teacher. __hey__ students are intelligent.

2. Mr. Johnson is a manager. *gerente* __his__ *Tienda* store is busy. *atareado*

3. Lisa and Bill are married. __Their__ apartment is big. *grande*

4. Claudia is a secretary. __her__ office is small.

5. Paul is a doctor. __hir__ x-rays are on the desk. *escritorio*

6. I am hungry. __my__ hamburger is good.

7. You are a taxi driver. __your__ car is yellow.

8. Monica and I are sick. __our__ medicine is not ready. *listo*
    enfermo

9. Mrs. Arabaci is sad. __her__ cat is lost.
    Triste *perder*

10. The boys are in the house. __Their__ toys are in the box.

Oral Exam

Student A

Student B

A: Hi. How are you?

B: Fine, thank you. And you?

A: Fine, thanks.

B: Where are you from?

A: I'm from Ecuador.
Whose umbrella is this?

B: It's my umbrella.

A: Here you are.

B: Thank you.

A: You're welcome. What day is today?

B: Today is Wednesday.
What's your phone number?

A: My phone number is area code (212) 555-1212.

B: How old are you?

A: I'm 23 years old.
What's this?

B: It's an eraser.

A: What do you do?

B: I'm a student.
Are you a teacher?

A: No, I'm not a teacher. I'm a student.
How do you say this in English?

B: A book.

A: Are you thirsty?

B: No, I'm not thirsty. I'm hungry.
How's the weather in Miami?

A: It's hot and humid.
What time is it?

B: It's 9:15.

A: I'm late. See you later.

B: Okay, bye.

What time do you work?

Lesson 6

Simple Present Tense
What time
When
Where

Actions
(Listen and repeat)

1. Dens

2. Drink

3. Drive

4. Kiss

5. Come

6. cry

7. Sleep

8. go home

9. Greet

10. wake up

11. write

12. walk

ZONI ENGLISH SYSTEM ©

13. Run

14. Read

15. buy

16. eat

17. Open

18. Sell

19. Cook

20. Close

21. Clean

22. wash

23. Wait

24. Sing

hope=esperanza

Please dance.

(Listen and do it)

Please drink
Please drive manejar
kiss
come
cry llorar
sleep
go
speak hablar
wake up
write
walk pasear
run correr

(Entire class participation)

ZONI ENGLISH SYSTEM ©

Match the vocabulary with the correct picture.

1. cook ___F___

2. wash ___H___
   lavay

3. write ___I___
   ai
   <escribi>

4. cry ___G___
   lloral

5. buy ___J___
   a
   comprav

6. sing ___B___

7. eat ___A___
   i
   comev

8. walk ___C___
   uoik

9. open ___D___

10. close ___E___

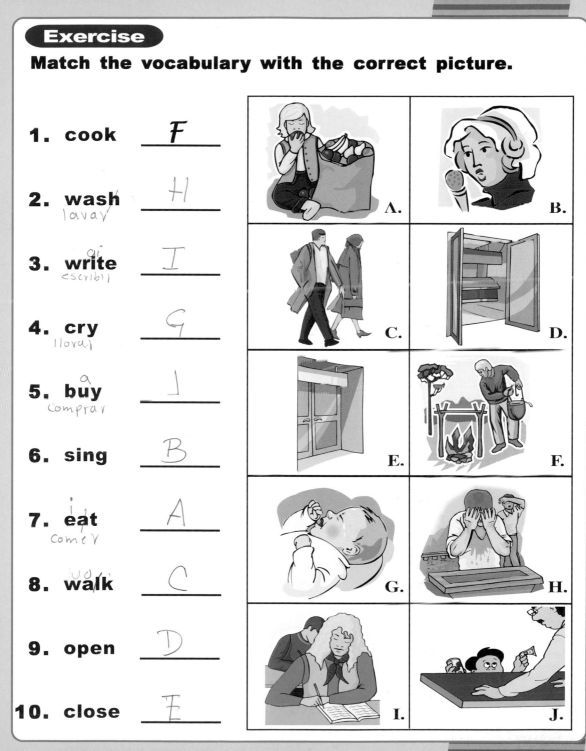

Bad Habits
(Listen and repeat)

I __Drink__ beer every day.

I __Smoke__ cigarettes every day.

I __Arrive__ late to school every day.

(cum1)

I __Eat__ a lot of fatty food every day.

I __Munch__ gum in the classroom every day.

(chew)

ZONI ENGLISH SYSTEM ©

Good Habits

(Listen and repeat)

I ___Drink___ water every day.

I ___Write___ my homework every day.
(Do)

I ___Study___ to school on time every day.
(come)

I ___Eat___ a lot of vegetables every day.

I ___Talk___ English in the classroom every day.
(Spoke)

Hello! Mr. Sanchez. How are you?

Group Work

Good habits

1. I run in park every day
2. I swim in the beach every day
3. I go to work in tha bicycle
4. I DO sport every day
5. I read a book every day

Bad habits

1. I smoke cigarettes every day
2. I drink coffee oll the day
3. I eat tangy (grasa) every day
4. I sleep in metre
5. arrive late in house

ZONI ENGLISH SYSTEM ©

Do you ...?   Yes, I ...
Yes, I do.

A: I eat lunch every day.
Do you eat lunch every day?

B: Yes, I eat lunch every day.
Yes, I do.

Interaction

A: I work in a hospital.
Do you work in a hospital?

B: Yes, I work in a hospital.
Yes, I do.

Pair Practice

A: I eat vegetables every day.

Do you eat vegetables ever? day

B: Yes, I eat vegetables ever day

yes, I do

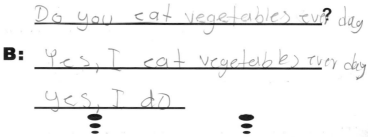

Performance

(Entire class participation)

Do you ...?   No, I don't ...
No, I don't.

A: I take the train every day.
Do you take the train every day?

B: No, I don't take the train every day.
No, I don't.
I take the bus every day.

Interaction

A: I speak Chinese every day.

Do you speak Chinese every day?

B: No, I don't speak <u>Chinese</u> every day.
No, I don't.
I speak English every day.

Pair Practice

A: I need $20.

Do <u>you need 20</u>?

B: <u>No, I don't need 20</u>
<u>No, I don't</u>
<u>I need $50</u>

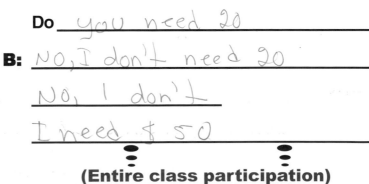

Performance

(Entire class participation)

Habits
(Listen and repeat)

| Do you...? | Yes, I do.
No, I don't. |

1. Do you <u>drink water</u> every day? **2.** Do you <u>smoke cigarettes</u> every day?

Yes, I do.   No, I don't.

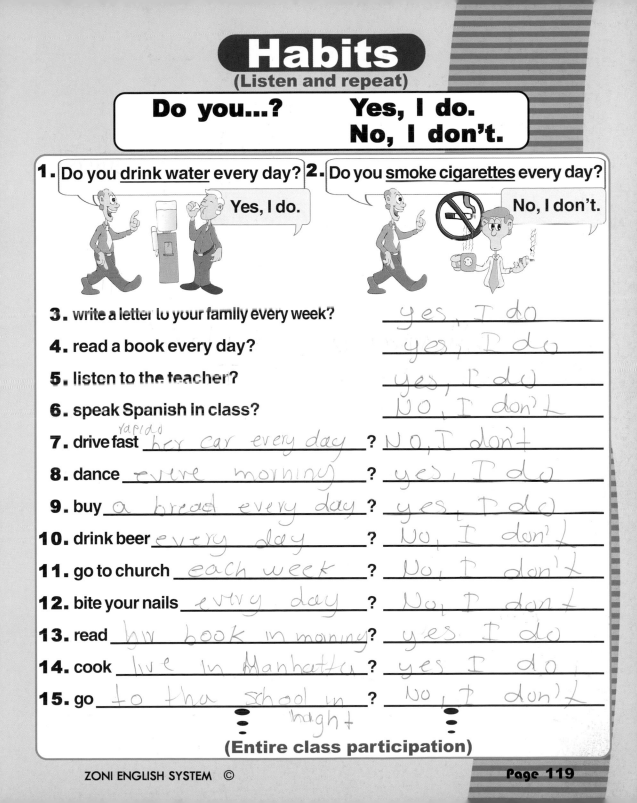

3. write a letter to your family every week? _yes, I do_

4. read a book every day? _yes, I do_

5. listen to the teacher? _yes, I do_

6. speak Spanish in class? _NO, I don't_

7. drive fast _her car every day_ (rapido) ? _NO, I don't_

8. dance _evere morning_ ? _yes, I do_

9. buy _a bread every day_ ? _yes, I do_

10. drink beer _every day_ ? _No, I don't_

11. go to church _each week_ ? _No, I don't_

12. bite your nails _evry day_ ? _No, I don't_

13. read _hir book in morning_ ? _yes I do_

14. cook _live in Manhattu_ ? _yes I do_

15. go _to tha school in_ ? _No, I don't_
haight

(Entire class participation)

Party Time !!

Walk around the classroom and ask
Do you ...?

N a m e
(no repetition)
(only "yes" answers)

1. live in ___Manhattan___ ? Norhely yes I do

2. like Rock and Roll? Tatta no I don't

3. take the bus every day? No I don't Anra

4. get up at 6:00? Yes I do Pedro

5. go to church every Sunday? No don't Berter

6. study computers? Yes I do Celso

7. eat Mexican food? Yes I do Oldanu

8. dance merengue? No Jea Jung

9. have breakfast every day? No I don't Andru

10. smoke every day? No I don't Alfred

11. live alone? No I don't Carly

Page 120   ZONI ENGLISH SYSTEM ©

Homework

Do you eat ice cream? No, I don't.

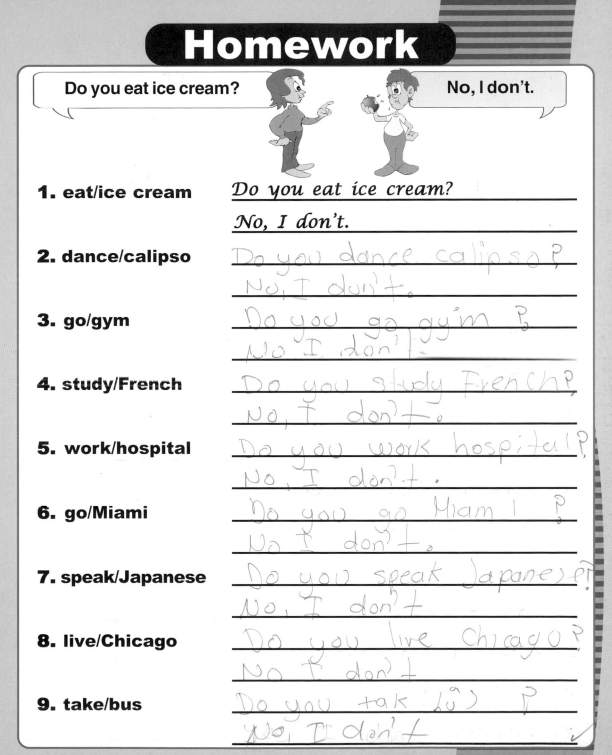

1. eat/ice cream

Do you eat ice cream?

No, I don't.

2. dance/calipso

Do you dance calipso?
No, I don't.

3. go/gym

Do you go gym?
No I don't.

4. study/French

Do you study French?
No, I don't.

5. work/hospital

Do you work hospital?
No, I don't.

6. go/Miami

Do you go Miami?
No I don't.

7. speak/Japanese

Do you speak Japanese?
No, I don't

8. live/Chicago

Do you live Chicago?
No I don't

9. take/bus

Do you tak bus?
No, I don't

What time

(Listen and repeat) apet

A: I get up at 6 o'clock.
7 o'clock.
8 o'clock.
9 o'clock.

B: What time do you get up?

A: At 6 o'clock.
At 7 o'clock.
At 8 o'clock.
At 9 o'clock.

Interaction

Pair Practice

A: I work at 8 o'clock.
B: What time do you work?
A: At 8 o'clock.

A: I study at 10 o'clock.
B: What time do you study?
A: At 10 o'clock.

Performance

A: I eat at 7 o'clock.
B: What time do you eat?
A: At 7 o'clock.

(Entire class participation)

ZONI ENGLISH SYSTEM ©

When

(Listen and repeat)

A: I play soccer every weekend.
I play soccer every day.
I play soccer every afternoon.
I play soccer every Sunday.

B: When do you play soccer?

A: Every weekend.
Every day.
Every afternoon.
Every Sunday.

Interaction

Pair Practice

A: I go to the park every Saturday.
B: When do you go to the park?
A: Every Saturday.

A: I drink coffee every morning.
B: When do you drink coffee?
A: Every morning.

Performance

A: I study English every night.
B: When do you study English?
A: Every night.

(Entire class participation)

Where

(Listen and repeat)

A: I live in New Jersey.
I live in Queens.
I live in Brooklyn.
I live in Manhattan.

B: Where do you live?

A: In New Jersey.
In Queens.
In Brooklyn.
In Manhattan.

Interaction

Pair Practice

A: I study in New York.
B: Where do you study?
A: In New York.

A: I work in New Jersey.
B: Where do you work?
A: In New Jersey.

Performance

A: I take the train to 34th street.
B: Where do you take the train?
A: To 34th street.

(Entire class participation)

Oral Practice

Make questions with your partner.

What time?

What time do you start class?

I start at noon.

1. study English?	1. At six o'clock.
2. eat lunch?	2. At noon.
3. get up?	3. At seven o'clock.
4. take the bus?	4. At ten o'clock.
5. go home?	5. At eight o'clock.

When?

When do you work?

I work every day.

1. play basketball?	1. Every weekend.
2. study computers?	2. Every Friday.
3. write letters?	3. Every week.
4. go to the beach?	4. Every summer.
5. see your family?	5. Every day.

Where?

Where do you live?

I live in Florida.

1. buy food?	1. In the supermarket.
2. play soccer?	2. In the park.
3. study?	3. At school.
4. relax?	4. At home.
5. eat lunch?	5. In the cafeteria.

Homework

Exercise A
Write sentences in the simple present. Use these verbs.

speak	study	work
like	finish	go
need	start *empezar*	eat
want *querer*	walk *paseo*	understand
show *espectaculo*	cook	come
live *vivo*	clean	read *leer*
watch *reloj*	open	write *escribir* rait

	Subject	verb
1.	I	speak English.
2.	They	study
3.	We	go in the park
4.	You	eat potatoes
5.	We	like ice cream
6.	They	need ids
7.	I	watch tv
8.	They	live in Mexico
9.	We	show dans
10.	You	open door
11.	I	finish homework
12.	We	walk
13.	You	cook beef
14.	They	work in hospital
15.	You	come in morning
16.	We	write letter
17.	You	
18.	I	understand Ingles
19.	We	clean glas
20.	They	They read book
21.	You	write

kiss   **sleep**   **cry**   **cook**

kiss	sleep	cry	cook
Kiss	Sleep	Cry	Cook
Kiss	Sleep	Cry	Cook
Kiss	Sleep	Cray	Cook
Kiss	Sleep	Cry	Cook
Kiss	Sleep	Cry	Cook
Kiss	Sleep	Cry	Cook
Kiss	Sleep	cry	Cook

drink   **walk**   **work**   **write**

drink	walk	work	write
drink	walk	work	write
drink	walk	Work	write
drink	walk	Work	write
drink	walk	Work	write
drink	walk	Work	write
drink	walk	Work	write
drink	walk	Work	write

1. I spiak inglish and fransh
   spic one eight

2. what time do you get to work

3. I live at 27 broad street

4. when Do you finish your Job

5. we Take the subway On 3 4 street

6. wher Do you Foot these books

7. they watch the movie every weekend

8. we eat aut every mronth

9. what Do you heed for your school

10. He walks in the park every night

Summary

Simple Present

AFFIRMATIVE	LIST OF VERBS

AFFIRMATIVE

I eat every day.
You eat every day.
He eats every day.
She eats every day.
It eats every day.
We eat every day.
You eat every day.
They eat every day.

NEGATIVE

I don't eat every day.
You don't eat every day.
He doesn't eat every day.
She doesn't eat every day.
It doesn't eat every day.
We don't eat every day.
You don't eat every day.
They don't eat every day.

QUESTIONS

Do I eat every day?
Do you eat every day?
Does he eat every day?
Does she eat every day?
Does it eat every day?
Do we eat every day?
Do you eat every day?
Do they eat every day?

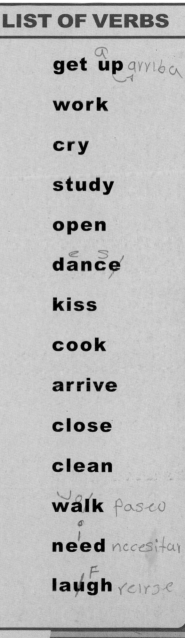

LIST OF VERBS

get up *arriba*

work

cry

study

open

dance *es*

kiss

cook

arrive

close

clean

walk *paseo*

need *necesitar*

laugh *reírse*

Oral Exam

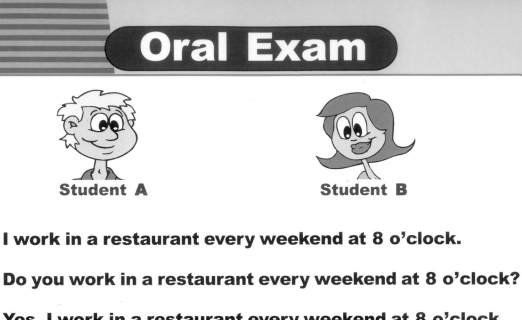

Student **A**   Student **B**

A: I work in a restaurant every weekend at 8 o'clock.

B: Do you work in a restaurant every weekend at 8 o'clock?

A: Yes, I work in a restaurant every weekend at 8 o'clock.

Yes, I do.

B: Do you work in a hospital every weekend at 8 o'clock?

A: No, I don't work in a hospital every weekend at 8 o'clock.

No, I don't.

B: Where do you work?

A: I work in a restaurant.

B: When do you work in the restaurant?

A: I work in the restaurant every weekend.

B: What time do you work in the restaurant?

A: I work in the restaurant every weekend at 8 o'clock.

ZONI ENGLISH SYSTEM ©

Lesson 7

There are some oranges.

There is/There are
Count/noncount Nouns
Some/Any

wan
happy
a
jogcorrer

Singular

There is a book on the chair.

There is ...

.
.
.

.
.
.

(Entire class participation)

Plural

There are five people in the class.

There are ...

.
.
.

.
.
.

There are five people in the class.

(Entire class participation)

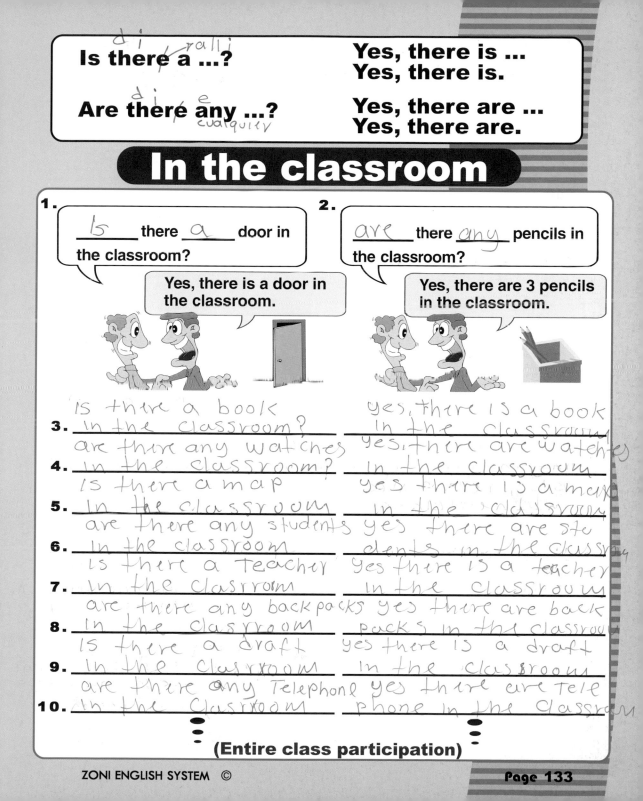

Is there a ...?

Yes, there is ...
Yes, there is.

Are there any ...?

Yes, there are ...
Yes, there are.

In the classroom

1. _Is_ there _a_ door in the classroom?

Yes, there is a door in the classroom.

2. _are_ there _any_ pencils in the classroom?

Yes, there are 3 pencils in the classroom.

3. Is there a book in the classroom? | yes, there is a book in the classroom

4. are there any watches in the classroom? | yes, there are watches in the classroom

5. Is there a map in the classroom | yes there is a map in the classroom

6. are there any students in the classroom | yes there are students in the classroom

7. Is there a Teacher in the classroom | yes there is a teacher in the classroom

8. are there any backpacks in the classroom | yes there are backpacks in the classroom

9. Is there a draft in the classroom | yes there is a draft in the classroom

10. are there any Telephone in the classroom | yes there are telephone in the classroom

(Entire class participation)

| Is there a ...? | No, there isn't a ...
No, there isn't. |
| Are there any ...? | No, there aren't any ...
No, there aren't. |

In the classroom

1. Is there a car in the classroom?

No, there isn't a car in the classroom.

2. Are there any doctors in the classroom?

No, there aren't any doctors in the classroom.

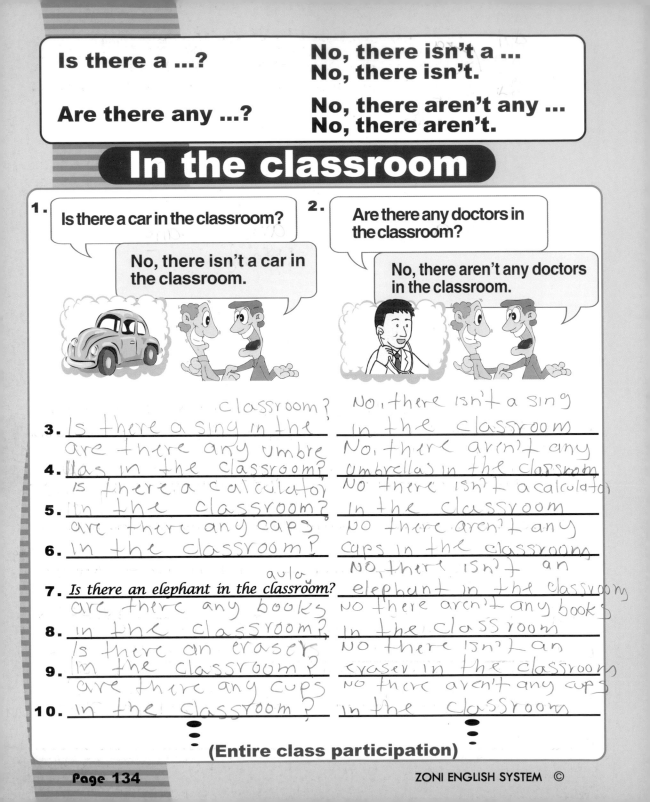

3. Is there a sing in the classroom?
No, there isn't a sing in the classroom

4. are there any umbrellas in the classroom?
No, there aren't any umbrellas in the classroom

5. Is there a calculator in the classroom?
No there isn't a calculator in the classroom

6. are there any caps in the classroom?
No there aren't any cups in the classroom

7. _Is there an elephant in the classroom?_ aula
No, there isn't an elephant in the classroom

8. are there any books in the classroom?
no there aren't any books in the classroom

9. Is there an eraser in the classroom?
No there isn't an eraser in the classroom

10. are there any cups in the classroom?
no there aren't any cups in the classroom

(Entire class participation)

ZONI ENGLISH SYSTEM ©

Homework

Make questions using objects in the picture.

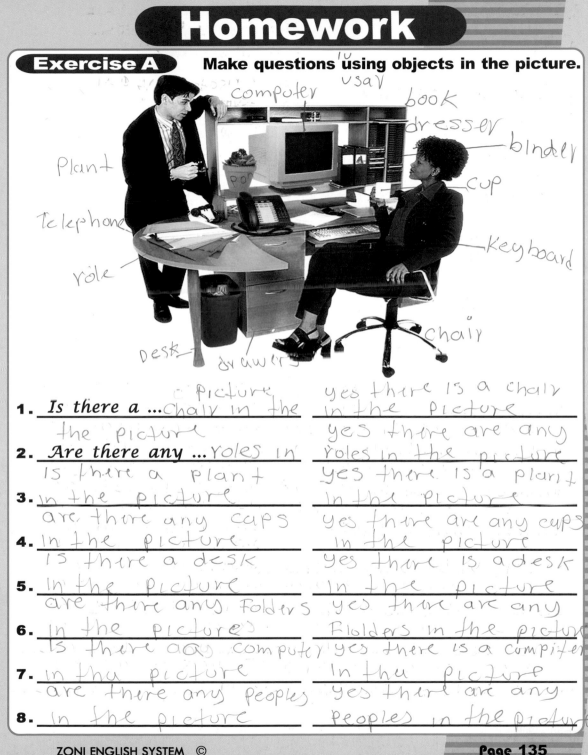

computer usa\
book
dresser
binder
Plant
cup
Telephone
keyboard
role
Desk
chair
drawers

1. *Is there a ...* chair in the picture   yes there is a chair in the picture
the picture
2. *Are there any ...* roles in   yes there are any roles in the picture
3. Is there a plant in the picture   yes there is a plant in the picture
4. are there any cups in the picture   yes there are any cups in the picture
5. Is there a desk in the picture   yes there is a desk in the picture
6. are there any folders in the picture   yes there are any folders in the picture
7. Is there aay computer in thu picture   yes there is a computer in thu picture
8. are there any peoples in the picture   yes there are any peoples in the picture

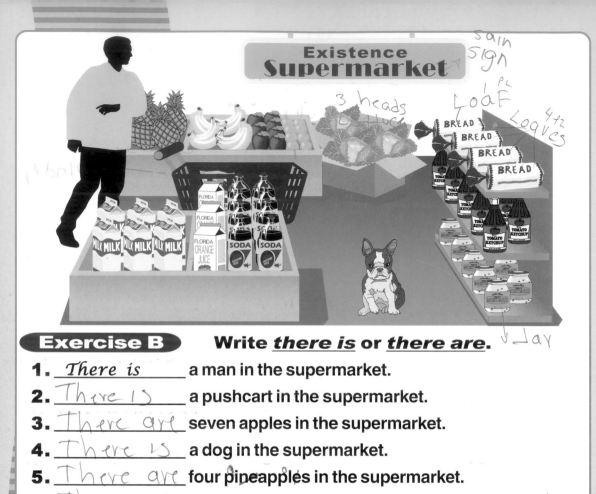

Existence
Supermarket

(handwritten annotations: "sain sign", "3 heads Lettuce", "1 PL LOAF Loaves 4+2", "grande ain", "Jay")

Exercise B — Write *there is* or *there are*.

1. *There is* a man in the supermarket.
2. *There is* a pushcart in the supermarket.
3. *There are* seven apples in the supermarket.
4. *There is* a dog in the supermarket.
5. *There are* four pineapples in the supermarket.
6. *There are* eight bottles of soda in the supermarket.
7. *There is* a big sign in the supermarket.
8. *There are* three heads of lettuce in the supermarket.
9. *There is* a box in the supermarket.
10. *There are* six containers of milk in the supermarket.

Exercise C — Check True or False.

	True	False
1. There is a woman in the supermarket.		F
2. There is a dog in the supermarket.	T	
3. There are televisions in the supermarket.		F
4. There are radios in the supermarket.		F
5. There are three men in the supermarket.		F

ZONI ENGLISH SYSTEM ©

Nouns

NONCOUNT	COUNT	
	Singular	**Plural**
milk	book	books
gas	stamp	stamps
salt	bag	bags
tea	shirt	shirts
Sugar	Pen	Pens
Coffee	bus	buses
fruit	car	cars
Soda	apple	apples
water	glass	glasses
homework	box	boxes

Existence in the classroom

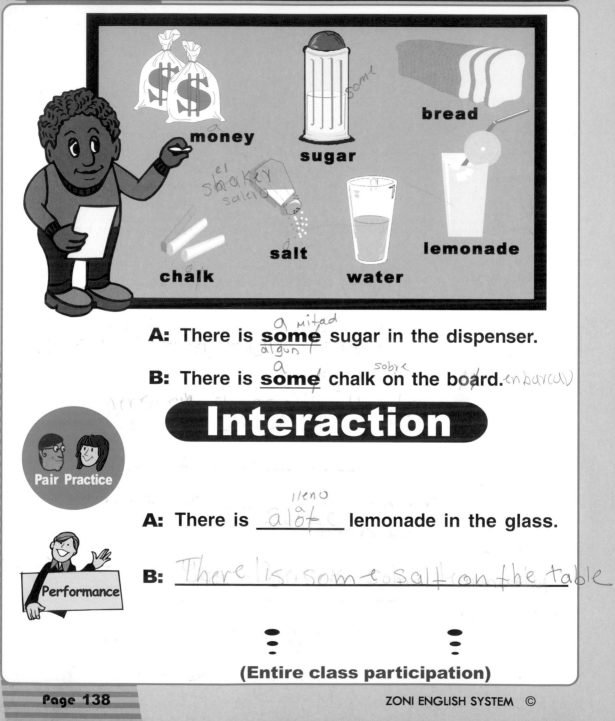

A: There is <u>**some**</u> sugar in the dispenser.

a mitad
algun

B: There is <u>**some**</u> chalk on the board.

a
sobre
en barra

Interaction

Pair Practice

A: There is ___*a lot*___ lemonade in the glass.

lleno

Performance

B: There is some salt on the table

(Entire class participation)

ZONI ENGLISH SYSTEM ©

Is there any ...?

Yes, there is ...
Yes, there is.

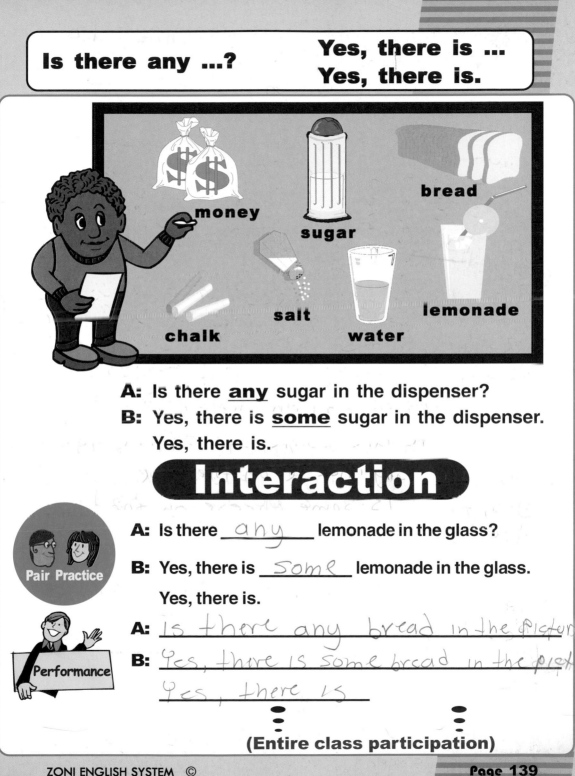

money

sugar

bread

chalk

salt

water

lemonade

A: Is there <u>**any**</u> sugar in the dispenser?

B: Yes, there is <u>**some**</u> sugar in the dispenser.
Yes, there is.

Interaction

Pair Practice

A: Is there ___any___ lemonade in the glass?

B: Yes, there is ___some___ lemonade in the glass.
Yes, there is.

Performance

A: Is there any bread in the picture?

B: Yes, there is some bread in the picture.
Yes, there is

(Entire class participation)

Homework

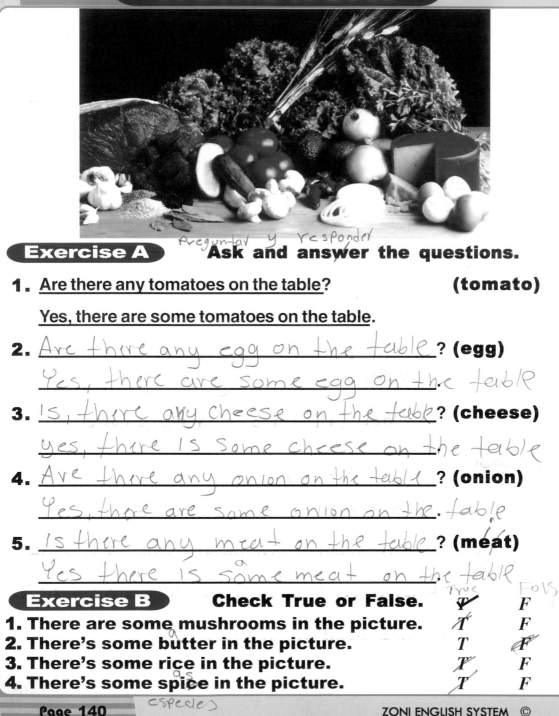

Preguntar y responder **Ask and answer the questions.**

1. <u>Are there any tomatoes on the table?</u>   **(tomato)**

   <u>Yes, there are some tomatoes on the table.</u>

2. <u>Are there any egg on the table</u>? **(egg)**
   <u>Yes, there are some egg on the table</u>

3. <u>Is, there any cheese on the table</u>? **(cheese)**
   <u>yes, there is some cheese on the table</u>

4. <u>Are there any onion on the table</u>? **(onion)**
   <u>Yes, there are some onion on the. table</u>

5. <u>Is there any meat on the table</u>? **(meat)**
   <u>Yes there is some meat on the table</u>

Exercise B   **Check True or False.**   True FOIS
                                                T   F

1. There are some mushrooms in the picture.   T   F
2. There's some butter in the picture.   T   F
3. There's some rice in the picture.   T   F
4. There's some spice in the picture.   T   F

especies)

Page 140   ZONI ENGLISH SYSTEM ©

Is there ~~algo~~ any ...?

No, there isn't any ...
No, there isn't.

A: Is there **any** sugar in the dispenser?
B: No, there isn't **any** sugar in the dispenser.
No, there isn't.

Interaction

Pair Practice

A: Is there any chalk on the board?

B: No, there isn't any chalk on the board.

No, there isn't.

Performance

A: Is there any lemonada in the glass?

B: No, there isn't any lemonada in the glass

No, there isn't

(Entire class participation)

Oral Practice
(Listen and repeat)

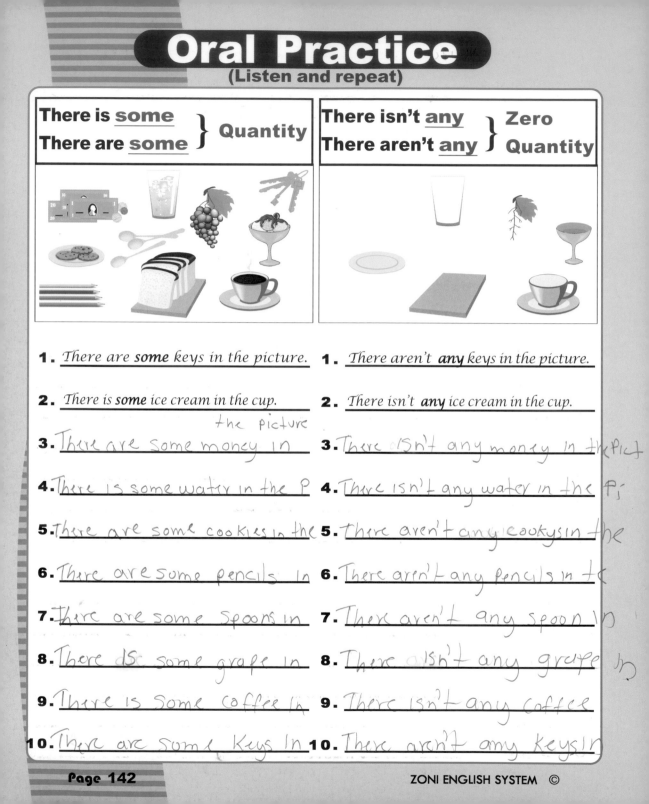

There is <u>some</u>	} Quantity	There isn't <u>any</u>	} Zero
There are <u>some</u>		There aren't <u>any</u>	Quantity

1. *There are **some** keys in the picture.*

2. *There is **some** ice cream in the cup.*

3. There are some money in the picture

4. There is some water in the P

5. There are some cookies in the

6. There are some pencils in

7. There are some spoons in

8. There is some grape in

9. There is some coffee in

10. There are some keys in

1. *There aren't **any** keys in the picture.*

2. *There isn't **any** ice cream in the cup.*

3. There isn't any money in the Pict

4. There isn't any water in the Pi

5. There aren't any cookys in the

6. There aren't any pencils in t

7. There aren't any spoon in

8. There isn't any grape in

9. There isn't any coffee

10. There aren't any keys in

ZONI ENGLISH SYSTEM ©

There is not any ...   There are not any ...
There isn't any ...   There aren't any ...

Look at the picture. Use *any* cualquiera   ~~en~~

1. cheese   There aren't any cheese in the
2. eggs   There aren't any eggs in the
3. tomato   There isn't any Tomato in the
4. sauce   There isn't any sauce in the
5. milk   There isn't any milk in the
6. knife _(cuchillo)_   There isn't any a knife in the
7. banana   There isn't any banana in the
8. cutting board   There isn't any cutting board in
9. bagel   There isn't any begel in the
10. rice   There isn't any rice in the
11. bacon   There isn't any bacon in the
12. tea   There isn't any tea in the
13. bread   There isn't any bread in the
14. butter   There isn't any butter in the

There are fifty states in the United States.
Florida is in the southern part of the United
States. There are a lot of nice beaches.
Minnesota is a very cold state. Minnesota is in
the northern part of the United States. There are
also many lakes in Minnesota. New York is on
the East coast. There are people from every
country in New York. California is on the West
coast. California is the home of Hollywood.

ZONI ENGLISH SYSTEM ©

Dictation 7

1. _____

2. _____

3. _____

4. _____

5. _____

6. _____

7. _____

8. _____

9. _____

10. _____

Homework

Change to the negative.

1. There are three students in my classroom.

There aren't any students in my classroom.

2. There are five teachers in the school.

There aren't any teachers in the school

3. There is some money in that bag.

There isn't any money in that bag

4. There are two books in the room.

There aren't any books in the room

5. There are seven pencils in the office.

There aren't any pencils in the office

6. There is some soda in the glass.

There isn't any soda in the glass

7. There is some milk in the refrigerator.

There isn't any milk in the refrigerator

8. There are twenty cars in the garage.

There arn't any cars in the garage

9. There is some rice on my plate.

There isn't any rice on my plate

10. There are thirty animals in the zoo.

There arn't any animals in the zoo

Exercise B Practice writing the following words.

seguir

Palabra

money	water	salt	sugar
money	water	Salt	Sugar
money	water	salt	Sugar
money	water	Salt	Sugar
money	water	salt	Sugar
money	water	Salt	Sugar
money	water	salt	Sugar
money	water	salt	Sugar

bread	pencil	fork	spoon
bread	Pencil	Fork	Spoon
bread	Pencil	Fork	Spoon
bread	Pencil	Fork	Spoon
bread	Pencil	Fork	Spoon
bread	Pencil	Fork	Spoon
bread	Pencil	Fork	Spoon
bread	Pencil	Fork	Spoon

Summary

	SINGULAR	PLURAL
Affirmative	**There is** **There's** *CONTRACTION*	**There are**
Question	**Is there a ...?** **Is there any ...?**	**Are there any ...?**
Negative	**There is not** **There isn't** *CONTRACTION*	**There are not** **There aren't** *CONTRACTION*
Negative / **Zero Quantity**	**There isn't any** *CONTRACTION*	**There aren't any** *CONTRACTION*

ZONI ENGLISH SYSTEM ©

Lesson 8

How many pears are there?

How many?
How much?
A little/some/a lot of
Much/many

How many ...?   There are ...

In the classroom

How many students are there in the classroom?

There are ___six___ students in the classroom.

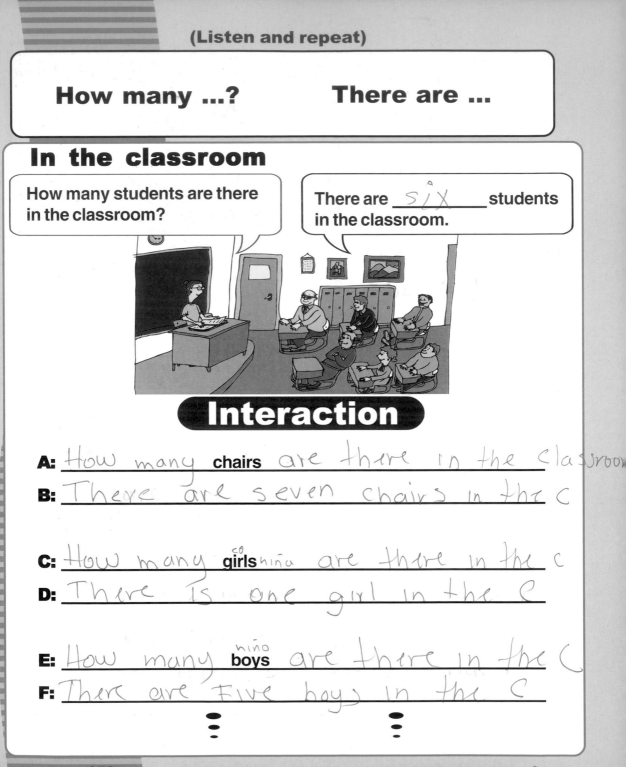

Interaction

A: How many **chairs** are there in the classroom

B: There are seven chairs in the c

C: How many **girls** niña are there in the c

D: There is one girl in the c

E: How many **boys** niño are there in the c

F: There are five boys in the c

li'ro

a little   some   a lot of

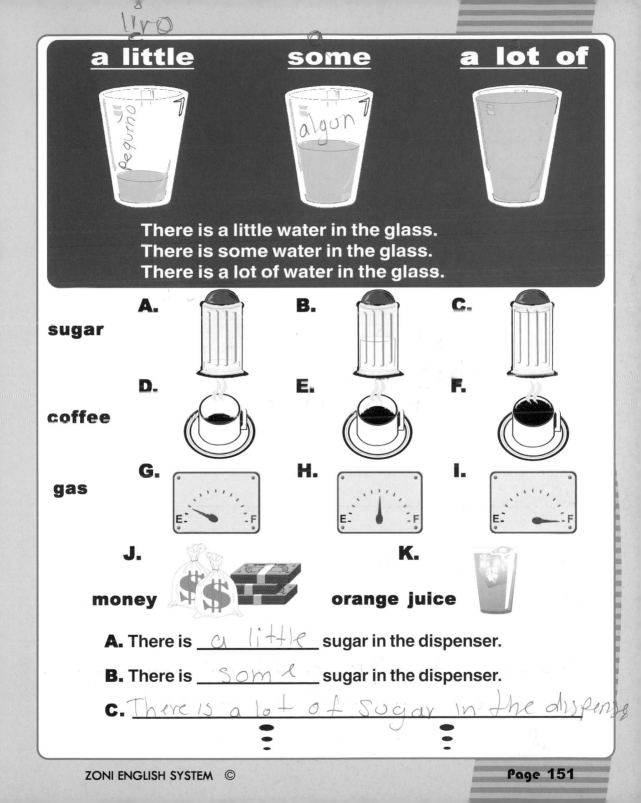

pequño   algun

There is a little water in the glass.
There is some water in the glass.
There is a lot of water in the glass.

sugar
    A.   B.   C.

coffee
    D.   E.   F.

gas
    G.   H.   I.

J.   **K.**

money   **orange juice**

A. There is ___a little___ sugar in the dispenser.

B. There is ___some___ sugar in the dispenser.

C. There is a lot of sugar in the dispense

How much ...?

There is a little ...
some
a lot of

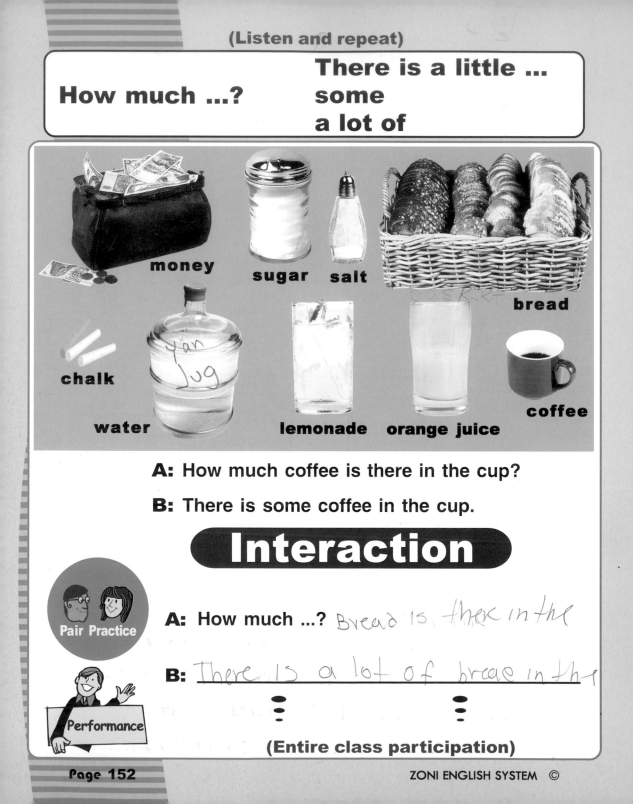

money

sugar   salt

bread

chalk

water

lemonade   orange juice

coffee

A: How much coffee is there in the cup?

B: There is some coffee in the cup.

Interaction

Pair Practice

A: How much ...? Bread is there in the

B: There is a lot of bread in the

(Entire class participation)

ZONI ENGLISH SYSTEM ©

Oral Practice
(Listen and repeat)

There's **a lot of**		Large *grande*
There are **a lot of**	}	quantity

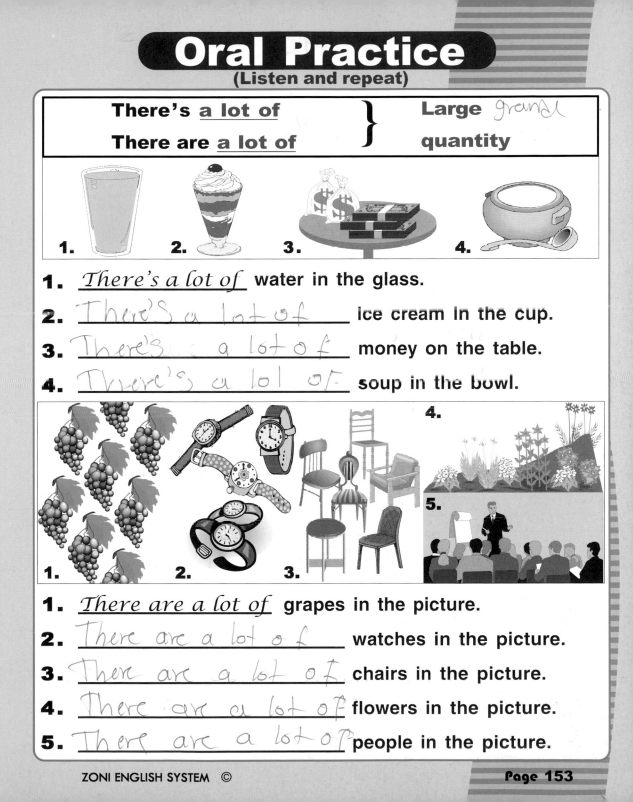

1. _There's a lot of_ water in the glass.
2. ___There's a lot of___ ice cream in the cup.
3. ___There's a lot of___ money on the table.
4. ___There's a lot of___ soup in the bowl.

1. _There are a lot of_ grapes in the picture.
2. ___There are a lot of___ watches in the picture.
3. ___There are a lot of___ chairs in the picture.
4. ___There are a lot of___ flowers in the picture.
5. ___There are a lot of___ people in the picture.

Oral Practice
(Listen and repeat)

| There isn't <u>much</u>
There aren't <u>many</u> | } | Small
quantity |

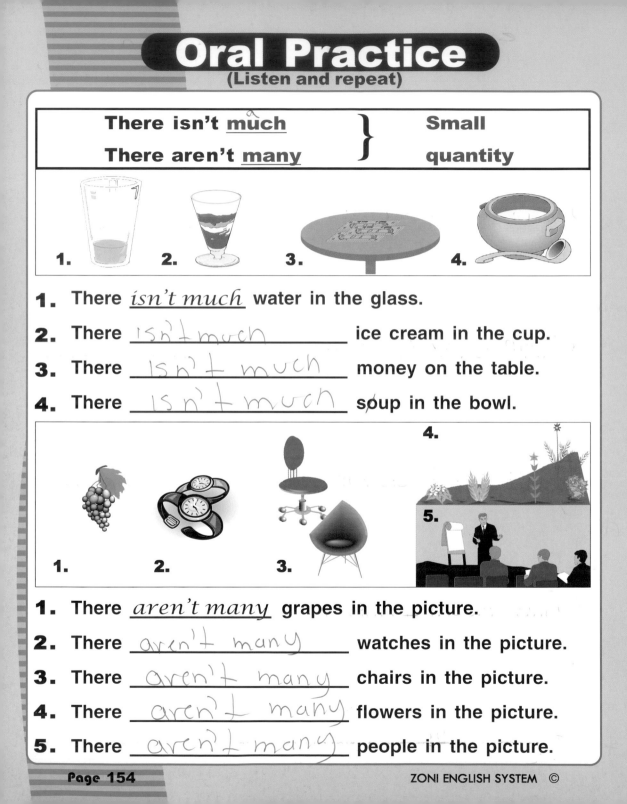

1. There _isn't much_ water in the glass.

2. There ___isn't much___ ice cream in the cup.

3. There ___isn't much___ money on the table.

4. There ___isn't much___ soup in the bowl.

1. There _aren't many_ grapes in the picture.

2. There ___aren't many___ watches in the picture.

3. There ___aren't many___ chairs in the picture.

4. There ___aren't many___ flowers in the picture.

5. There ___aren't many___ people in the picture.

ZONI ENGLISH SYSTEM ©

1. There isn't much ~~grapes~~ ^{bread} grapes in the kitchen

2. How much soup is there in tha pot

3. There are some cuares in the (coinfci) ^{guarters,} Purse ^{pen}

4. There aren't any visitor in the lovill ^{lobby}

5. How ~~much~~ ^{many bottles of} patus juise are there in the refrigerator

Homework

Exercise A   Change to the negative: Use _any_.

1. I want some change.

   I don't want any change.

2. You need some sugar.

   you need any sugar

3. We cook some chicken.

   we don't cook any ch

4. You give me some help.

   yo don't give me any

5. They clean some rooms.

   They don't clean any rooms

6. I read some magazines.

   I don't read any m

7. We drink some wine.

   We don't drink any

8. I receive some mail.

   I don't receive any

9. They watch some movies.

   They don't watch any

10. I eat some french fries.

    I don't eat any French

11. You need some paper.

    You don't need any

12. I wash some clothes on Fridays.

    I don't wash any

13. I know some Chinese.

    I don't know any

14. You bake some cookies.

    Yo don't bake any

15. There is some heat in the apartment.

    There isn't is any heat

Exercise B

Change to the negative: Use _much_ and _many_.

1. I need a lot of paper. _I don't need much paper._

2. I work with a lot of people. I don't work with much *(many)*

3. They wash a lot of dishes. They don't *many* wash much *(many)*

4. You have a lot of money in the bank. You don't have much

5. I go to a lot of parties. I don't go to much *(many)*

6. I put a lot of fruit in the bowl. I don't put much

7. You write a lot of letters to him. You don't write much *(many)*

8. They give a lot of presents. They don't give much *(many)*

9. I know a lot of Spanish. I don't know much

10. They put a lot of salt in my food. They don't put much

11. I work a lot of hours. I don't work much *(many)*

12. I eat a lot of french fries. I don't eat much

13. You receive a lot of mail every day. You don't receive much

14. We read a lot of books. we don't read much

15. There's a lot of snow on the street. There   much

ZONI ENGLISH SYSTEM ©

Exercise C   Complete the sentences.

1. There's a lot of ___bread___ in the supermarket.

2. There's a lot of ___Milk___ in the refrigerator.

3. There are a lot of ___Spices___ in the kitchen.

4. There are a lot of ___Families___ in this neighborhood. vecindario

5. There's a lot of ___Money___ in the bank.

6. There are a lot of ___Books___ in the classroom.

7. There's a lot of ___bread___ in the bakery. Panaderia

8. There are a lot of ___Dogs___ in the zoo.

9. There's a lot of ___Juice___ in the glass.

10. There's a lot of ___coffee___ in the cup.

11. There aren't many ___Cars___ in the garage.

12. There are a lot of ___Flowers___ in the park.

13. There isn't much ___pleit___ on the table.

14. There aren't many ___pipols___ in New York.

15. There are a lot of ___Roles___ in the office.

ZONI ENGLISH SYSTEM ©

Lesson 9

Where is your house?

Prepositions
Ordinal Numbers
Health
Directions and Locations
Registration Form

Everybody Do It!

(Listen and repeat)

#1 **#2**

1. Take out a piece of paper. *Fuera* *a* *Pedazo* *Papel*

2. Crumple it up.

3. Put it on your desk. *Escritorio*

4. Put it under your desk. *a debajo*

5. Put it in your pocket. *dentro* *a* *bolsillo*

6. Put it in front of your feet. *pie*

7. Put it under your book. *a debajo*

8. Put it behind your desk. *a por detras*

9. Put it in your pocket again. *bolsillo* *otra vez*

ZONI ENGLISH SYSTEM ©

(Listen and repeat)

On

Sobre

The phone is __On__ the desk.

The books are __On__ the desk.

The book is __On__ the chair.

The keys are __On__ the chair.

Under

Debajo

The phone is __Under__ the desk.

The books are __Under__ the desk.

The book is __Under__ the chair.

The keys are __Under__ the chair.

KISS

(Listen and repeat)

In	In front of	Behind

The book is __in__ the briefcase.

The motorcycle is __in front of__ the bus.

The motorcycle is __behind__ the bus.

The books are __In__ the briefcase.

The cars are __In fron of__ the bus.

The cars are __Behind__ the bus.

The fire extinguisher is __In__ the box.

The banana is __In front of__ the apple.

The banana is __Behind__ the apple.

The fire extinguishers are __In__ the box.

The bananas are __In front of__ the orange.

The bananas are __Behind__ the orange.

ZONI ENGLISH SYSTEM ©

Do it!
Interaction

Where is the book?	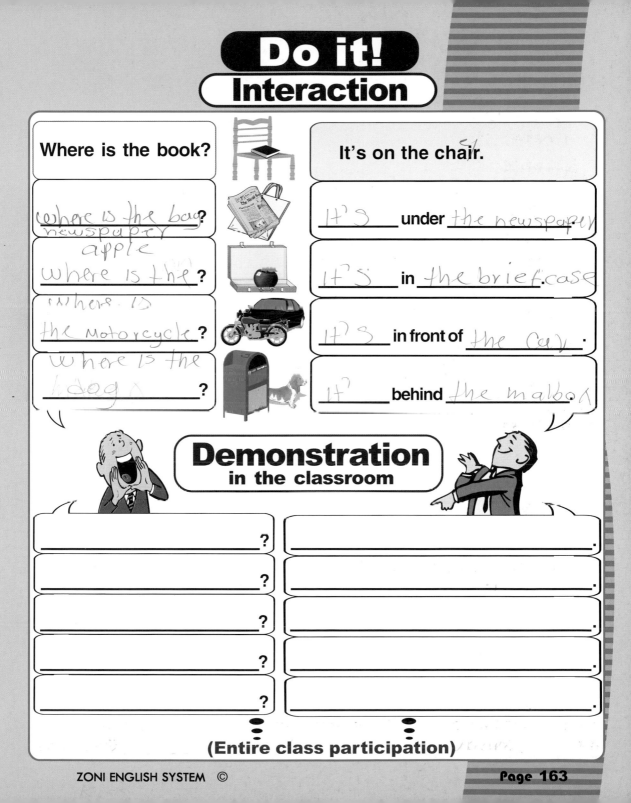	It's on the chair.

Where is the bag?
newspaper

It's under the newspaper

apple
Where is the ?

It's in the brief case

where is the Motorcycle?

It's in front of the car.

Where is the dog ?

It behind the mailbox

Demonstration
in the classroom

?	.
?	.
?	.
?	.
?	.

(Entire class participation)

The Kitchen Table

Where is the knife?

1. The knife is on the plate.

2. The knife is in the glass.

3. The knife is under the bread.

4. The knife is behind the soda.

5. The knife is in front of the milk.

Student A

Where is the knife?

Where is the fork?

Where is the spoon?

Where is the napkin? *a*

cat

fly

mouse

dog

Student B

Where is the cat? *on Table*

Where is the dog? *under chair*

Where is the mouse? *behind plant*

Where is the fly? *in glass*

knife

spoon

napkin

fork

ZONI ENGLISH SYSTEM ©

Do it!
in the classroom

next to

Where's Martha?

She's <u>next to</u> Christopher.

Martha

Christopher

behind

Where's Paula?

She's <u>behind</u> Tim.

Tim

Paula

in front of

Where's John?

He's <u>in front of</u> Susan.

John

Susan

(Entire class participation)

teeth   mouth   tooth   bath

(Listen and repeat)

1st	first	11th	eleventh
2nd	second	12th	twelfth
3rd	third	13th	thirteenth
4th	fourth	14th	fourteenth
5th	fifth	15th	fifteenth
6th	sixth	16th	sixteenth
7th	seventh	17th	seventeenth
8th	eighth	18th	eighteenth
9th	ninth	19th	nineteenth
10th	tenth	20th	twentieth

30th	thirtieth
40th	fortieth
50th	fiftieth
60th	sixtieth
70th	seventieth
80th	eightieth
90th	ninetieth

Pronunciation Practice

13th	30th	17th	70th
14th	40th	18th	80th
15th	50th	19th	90th
16th	60th		

ZONI ENGLISH SYSTEM ©

Where do you live?

(Listen and repeat)

I live **on** Bergenline Avenue.

on

I live **on** Bergenline Ave. **between** 1st and 2nd streets.

en medio de

between

I live **next to** the supermarket.

SUPERMARKET

next to

I live **on the corner.**

esquina

on the corner

ZONI ENGLISH SYSTEM ©

Page 169

Emergency

Reasons we call

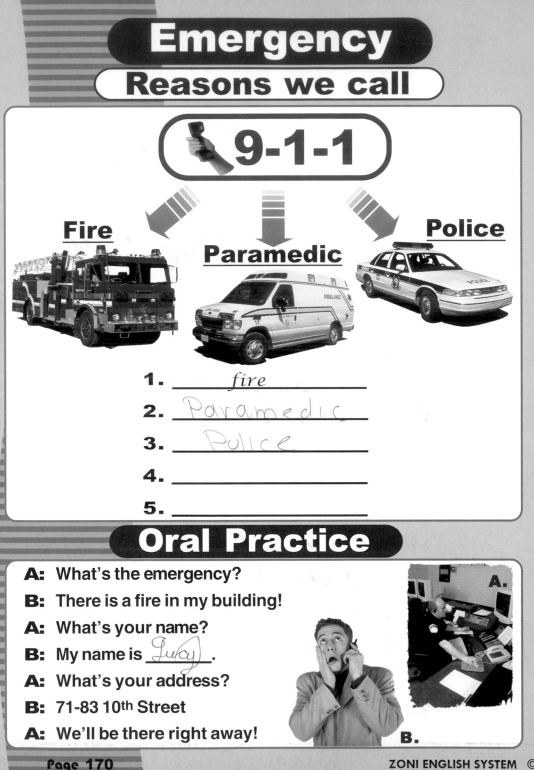

📞 **9-1-1**

Fire

Paramedic

Police

1. _____*fire*_____
2. _____Paramedic_____
3. _____Police_____
4. _____
5. _____

Oral Practice

A: What's the emergency?

B: There is a fire in my building!

A: What's your name?

B: My name is _Lucy_.

A: What's your address?

B: 71-83 10th Street

A: We'll be there right away!

A.

B.

Doctor says ...

(Listen and do it)

Roll up your sleeves

Open your mouth

Say "aah"

Cough *toser*

Breath in *respirar*

Hold your breath *detener aire*

Breath out *sacar el aire*

Look up

Look down

Make a fist *puño mano*

Relax

Health
(Listen and repeat)
I have...

pain

1. I have a (pain) headache

2. I have the finger a cut in hand

3. I have an allergy

4. I have a backache

5. I have a Fever

6. I have a cold

7. I have a stomachache

8. I have a Fracture

9. I have a Sunburn

10. I have a muscle pain

11. I twisted sprain

12. I catch a cold / Flu / runny nose

ZONI ENGLISH SYSTEM ©

catch a cold

Oral Practice

A: I have <u>a broken leg</u>.
B: Get a cast.

some ointment

a shot

some aloe vera

crutches

some aspirin

an ice pack

a massage

a cast

a band aid

acupuncture

some medicine

some rest

Directions and Locations

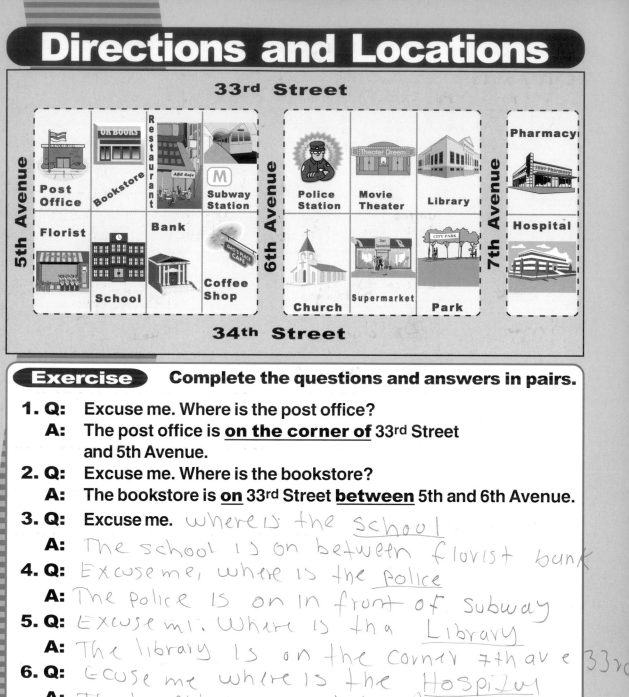

33rd Street

Post Office | Bookstore | Restaurant | Subway Station

Florist | School | Bank | Coffee Shop

5th Avenue | 6th Avenue

Police Station | Movie Theater | Library

Church | Supermarket | Park

7th Avenue

Pharmacy | Hospital

34th Street

Exercise — **Complete the questions and answers in pairs.**

1. Q: Excuse me. Where is the post office?
A: The post office is **on the corner of** 33rd Street and 5th Avenue.

2. Q: Excuse me. Where is the bookstore?
A: The bookstore is **on** 33rd Street **between** 5th and 6th Avenue.

3. Q: Excuse me. where is the school
A: The school is on between florist bank

4. Q: Excuse me, where is the police
A: The police is on in front of subway

5. Q: Excuse me. Where is tha Library
A: The library is on the corner 7th ave 33rd

6. Q: Ecuse me where is the Hospital
A: The hospital is on behind the pharmacy

Student A

Find: the restaurant, the church, the pharmacy, the movie theater, the hospital, the school, the library, the florist.

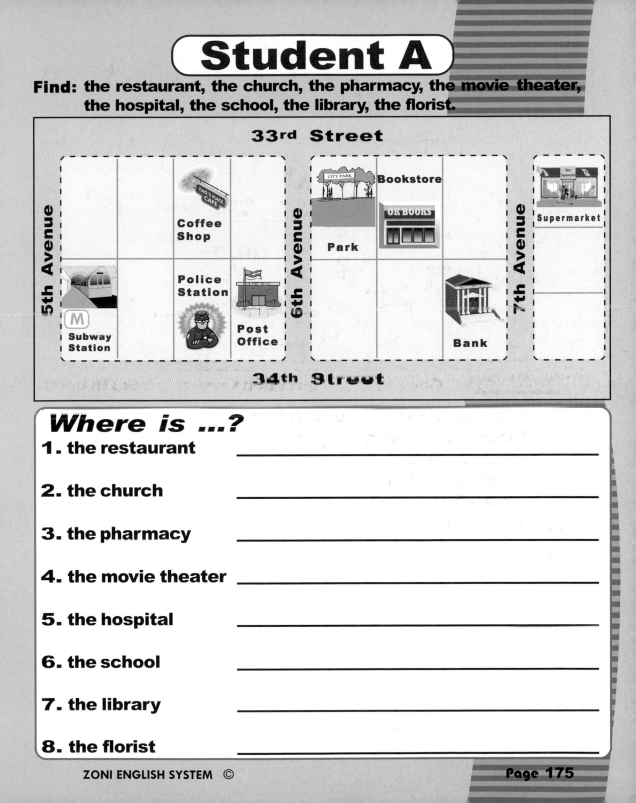

Where is ...?

1. the restaurant _____

2. the church _____

3. the pharmacy _____

4. the movie theater _____

5. the hospital _____

6. the school _____

7. the library _____

8. the florist _____

Student B

Find: the park, the supermarket, the post office, the coffee shop, the subway station, the bank, the police station, the bookstore.

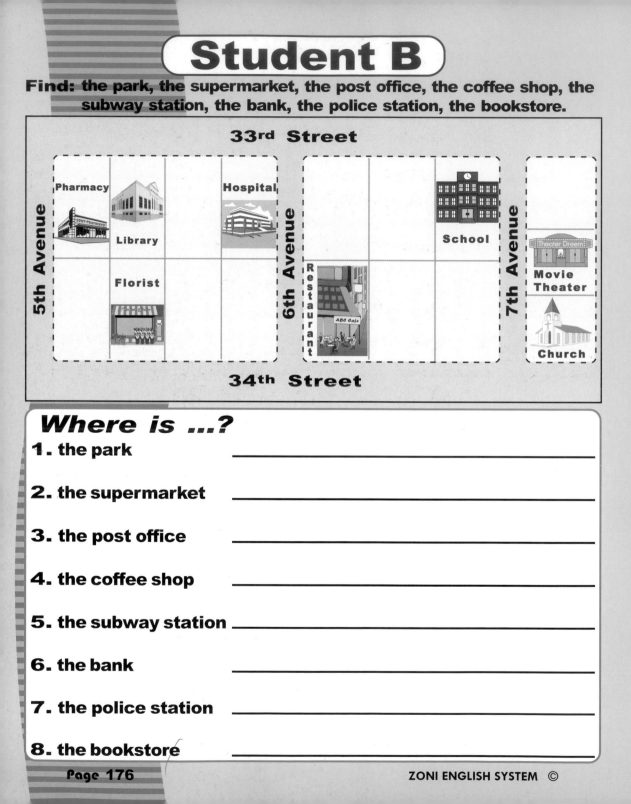

Where is ...?

1. the park _____

2. the supermarket _____

3. the post office _____

4. the coffee shop _____

5. the subway station _____

6. the bank _____

7. the police station _____

8. the bookstore _____

Homework

Registration Form
ZONI LANGUAGE CENTERS

Name _Lopez_ _John_
Last   First

Address _74-03 Broadway Ave. Apt. 11_

City _Jackson Heights_ **State** _NY_ **Zip code** _11372_

Home phone _(718) 564-3897_

Work phone _(212) 345 0998_

Date of birth _04_ _22_ _75_
     month   day   year

Registration Form
ZONI LANGUAGE CENTERS

eta

Name _Garcia_ _Ma de la Luz_
Last   First

Address _415 West Th 59 Street_

City _New York_ **State** _N.Y_ **Zip code** _10019_

Home phone _(212) 5416906_

Work phone _(212) 5416906_

Date of birth _08_ _14_ _66_
August _Fourteen_ _1966_
     month   day   year

Group Work

Reasons to go to the next level

1. <u>To learn to speak in the past tense</u>

2. <u>To learn a lot of new vocabulary</u>

3. _____

4. _____

5. _____

6. _____

7. _____

8. _____

CONGRATULATIONS!
Welcome to the next level.

ZONI™ ENGLISH SYSTEM 2

Summary
Prepositions

<u>On</u> the chair
Sobre

<u>In front of</u> the chair
Frente

<u>Under</u> the chair
a
debajo

<u>Behind</u> the chair
biaind
Por detras

<u>In</u> the box
dentro

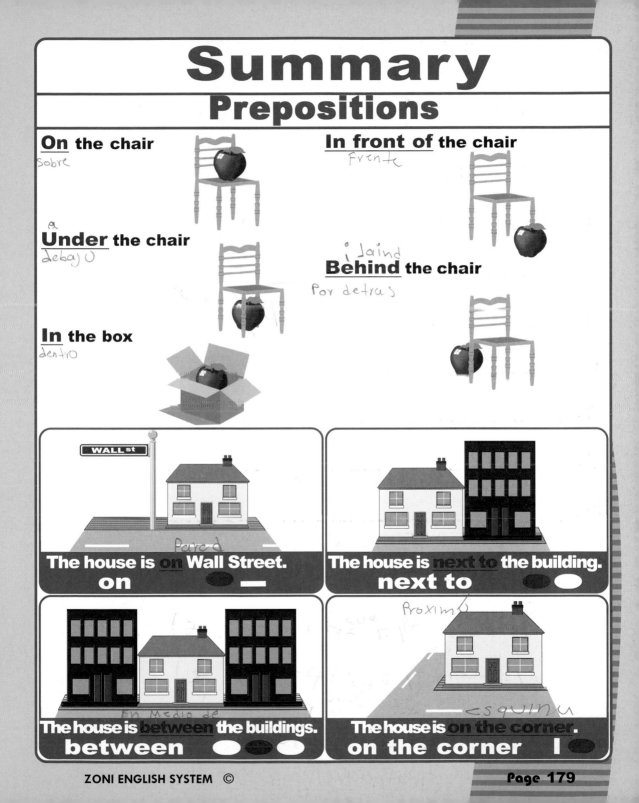

The house is <u>on</u> Wall Street.
on   ⬤ ▬

The house is <u>next to</u> the building.
next to   ⬤ ⬜

Pared

The house is <u>between</u> the buildings.
between   ⬤ ⬤ ⬜

En medio de

The house is <u>on the corner</u>.
on the corner   ⬤
Proximo
esquina

Final Oral Exam

Student A

Student B

A: Hi. How are you?

B: Fine, thank you. And you?

A: Fine, thanks.

B: Where are you from?

A: I'm from Mexico. What's your last name?

B: My last name is Ruiz.

A: Spell it, please.

B: R - U - I - Z. Where do you live?

A: I live on Bergenline Avenue. How old are you?

B: I'm 19 years old.

A: What day is today?

B: Today is Monday.

A: Are you cold?

B: No, I'm not cold. I'm hot.

A: Do you work?

B: Yes, I work.

A: What do you do?

B: I'm a waitress. camarera

A: Do you take the bus every day?

B: No, I don't take the bus. I take the train. Where's the umbrella?

A: The umbrella is under the chair. What's this?

B: That's a book. Whose book is that? Jus

A: That's my book. aquel

B: Is there a post office on Main Street?

A: No, there isn't a post office on Main Street. What time is it?

B: It's 9:50.

A: Oh no! I'm late! See you later.

B: Bye. examen

That aquel

ZONI ENGLISH SYSTEM ©

Appendix

Verbs

de quién
¡¡ quiénes)
whose cuyo.

There allí
allá
ahí

why por qué
who quién
quienes

VERBS

answer responder | feel sentir | live vivo | sit sentarse
arrive llegar | fight combatir | look mirar | sleep dormir
ask preguntar | find hallar | lose perder | speak hablar
become convertirse | finish acabar | love | spend gastar
begin empezar | fit ir bien | make hacer | stand de pie
blow soplar | fix | meet encontrar | start empezar
borrow | fly volar mosca | miss echar de menos | stop parar
bring traer | forget olvidar | mix mezclar | study estudiar
buy comprar | get conseguir | need necesitar | swim nadar
call amar | get up | open | take tomar
carry llevar | give dar | paint pintura | teach instruir
catch capturar | go ir | play jugar | think pensar
clean limpio | grow crecer | practice practica | understand
close serrar | hate odio | pray rezar | visit
come venir | have tener | push empujar | wake
cook cocinar | help ayudar | rain lluvia | walk paseo
cost precio | hurry | read leer | want querer
cry llorar | invite invito | rent alquilar | wash lavar
cut cortar | jump saltar | repeat repetir | watch reloj
dance bailar | kiss ves | rest desansar | wear llevar
decide decir | know saber | ride montar | whistle silbato
discuss discutir | laugh reirse | run correr | win ganar
do hacer | leave dejar | say decir | wink
drink bebida | let permitir | see ver | work
drive conducir | lie mentir | sell vender | write escribir
eat comer | like gustar | send enviar |
fall otoño | listen escuchar | sing cantar |